ZAP!

Television is art in this tower of 1,003 screens, designed by video artist Nam Jung-paik and exhibited in Seoul, South Korea. The name of the sculpture is *The More, the Better.* AP/Wide World Photos

ZAP!

A Brief
History of
Television

by
Marian Calabro

Four Winds Press ⚡ New York
Maxwell Macmillan Canada   Toronto
Maxwell Macmillan International   New York   Oxford   Singapore   Sydney

Four Winds Press
Macmillan Publishing Company
866 Third Avenue
New York, NY 10022

Maxwell Macmillan Canada, Inc.
1200 Eglinton Avenue East
Suite 200
Don Mills, Ontario M3C 3N1

Macmillan Publishing Company is
part of the Maxwell Communica-
tion Group of Companies.

First edition
Printed and bound in the United
States of America

10 9 8 7 6 5 4 3 2 1

The text of this book is set
in Bauer Bodoni.

Book design by Christy Hale

Library of Congress
Cataloging-in-Publication Data
Calabro, Marian.
Zap! : a brief history of television /
Marian Calabro.—1st ed.
    p.   cm.
Includes bibliographical refer-
ences and index.
Summary: Surveys the history of
television and the different kinds
of programs broadcast, including
situation comedies, dramas, and
children's television.
ISBN 0-02-716242-7
1. Television broadcasting—
History—Juvenile literature.
[1. Television broadcasting—
History.] I. Title.
PN1992.2.C34   1992
384.55'4'09—dc20   91-744

PERMISSIONS 〰〰〰〰〰〰〰〰

Grateful acknowledgment is made for permission to reprint from the following copyrighted
works:

The Cool Fire by Bob Shanks. Copyright ©
1976 by Comco Productions. New York: W. W.
Norton, 1976.

Inside Prime Time by Todd Gitlin. New York:
Pantheon Books, 1983, 1985. (For quote from
Grant Tinker.)

"Mister Ed." Words and music by Jay Livingston and Ray Evans. Copyright © 1960 Jay
Livingston Music and St. Angelo Music. Rights
of St. Angelo Music administered by MCA Music Publishing, A Division of MCA Inc., New
York, N.Y. 10019. Copyright renewed. All
rights reserved. Used by permission.

*Selling America's Kids: Commercial Pressures
on Kids of the 90's.* Copyright © 1990 by
Consumers Union of United States, Inc., Yon-
kers, N.Y. 10703. Excerpted by permission
from CONSUMER REPORTS, August 1990.

Television by Michael Winship. New York:
Random House, 1988. (For quotes from J. P.
Miller, Steven Bochco, David Wolper, Peter
Marthesheimer, Harry Coyle, and Arthur C.
Clarke.)

"We Are the Men of Texaco." Copyright ©
1948 Texaco Inc.

"Where Everybody Knows Your Name" by
Gary Portnoy and Judy Hart Angelo. Copyright
© 1982 by Addax Music Co., Inc.

For my mother, Marion Montagnoli Calabro, who showed me early in life that it's possible to be both a fan and a critic of television at the same time. And for Cindy Kane, the godmother of this book.

ACKNOWLEDGMENTS

Television literally changes before our eyes, and making sense of its larger patterns in a book of this length was both fun and challenging. I thank these industry insiders for sharing their knowledge: Arianna Licet Ariza of the National Cable Television Association; Red Barber, the dean of sports broadcasters; Charlotte Baecher, director of Consumers Union's Educational Services Division; Jack Breslin of STF Productions, Inc., a subsidiary of Fox Television; Frances Buch, who generously recalled her early years at CBS; Peggy Charren, founder of Action for Children's Television; Kassaye Damena, former program director of Ethiopian Television; Rob Deigh, director of corporate information, Public Broadcasting Service; Jennifer Lawson, PBS executive vice president and programming chief; Chuck Kraemer, essayist and critic at WCVB-TV in Boston; Andy Lippman, associate director of the New Media Lab at the Massachusetts Institute of Technology; Trav Livingston, daughter of TV theme-song master Jay Livingston, who shared tidbits from the era of "Mr. Ed"; Bill Morris, former WNBC-TV news producer and current sports producer; and Dorothy Swanson, founder and president of Viewers for Quality Television.

Special thanks go to the staff of the Museum of Television and Radio, where I had the opportunity to hear and question several of the most influential people in television: Walter Cronkite; David Davis, president and executive director of "American Playhouse"; screenwriter Horton Foote; CBS news veterans Don Hewitt and Richard C. Hottelet; CNN correspondent Brian Jenkins; Joan Konner, dean of the Graduate School of Journalism, Columbia University; Fred Silverman, prime-time program producer and former network executive; Brandon Stoddard, president of ABC Productions; Jac Venza, director of performance programming for PBS member station WNET/13 in New York; Richard Wald, senior vice president, ABC News; and the cast and creators of "Murphy Brown."

I am also grateful to J. Fred MacDonald, eminent broadcast historian, who reviewed the manuscript and made valuable suggestions, and to Diana M. Guerriero, who helped with the photo research.

At Four Winds Press, I enjoyed the support of Virginia Duncan, Christy Hale, Katherine Kirkpatrick, and SoYung Pak. At home, I was nurtured by endless encouragement from Bernie Libster, who shares our household's only television set.

CONTENTS

〜〜〜〜〜〜〜〜〜〜〜〜〜〜〜〜〜〜〜〜〜〜〜〜〜〜〜〜〜〜

Introduction: *The Power of Television*   xi
1. The World of Tomorrow: *Inventing Television*   3
2. Lots of Laughs: *Variety and Situation Comedy*   16
3. Sometimes Serious: *Drama, Action/Adventure,*
   Docudrama, TV Movies   35
4. Night and Day: *Daytime Programs, Soap Operas,*
   Game Shows, Talk Shows   51
5. May the Best Image Win: *News and Politics*   66
6. Victory and Defeat: *Sports and the Olympics*   86
7. Small Things Considered: *Children's Television*   99
8. The Business Side: *Advertisers, Programming,*
   Ratings   115
9. Quality and Quantity: *Public Television*
   and Cable Television   130
10. Good Morning, World: *International Television*   147
11. The Boob Tube: *The Case Against Television*   161
12. Into the Twenty-first Century: *The Future*
    of Television   173
Appendix 1 *Top-Rated Prime-Time Programs*   185
Appendix 2 *Some Emmy Award Winners*   189
Appendix 3 Key Network and Cable Addresses   195
Select Bibliography   197
Suggestions for Young Readers   199
Index   201

*"Don't you understand? This is life, this is
what is happening. We can't switch to another channel."*

Drawing by Robert Day.

INTRODUCTION:

The Power of Television

*T*elevision is a mega-invention. Like electricity, cars, and telephones, it has changed the routines of daily life. It affects how we speak, dress, learn, vote, and relax; most people can't imagine living without it. Some studies say television even influences how we think.

Yet television itself *does* nothing. It is not a dictator or brainwasher. It does not turn itself on and off. Television is no better or worse than the people behind it and the people in front of it—the people who choose the programs and the people who watch those programs.

In the 1960s, when television had become a fact of life in most homes around the world, it was fashionable to say that "the medium is the message." That view, put forward by Canadian professor Marshall McLuhan, makes the *idea* of television more important than individual programs. It means that everything on television has roughly the same reality, whether it is a presidential press conference or "The Simpsons." Considering that half of American viewers turn on their sets with no particular program in mind, McLuhan may have been half right.

However, other viewers demand more. They watch television programs, not television itself. They like good shows of all kinds: good comedies, dramas, news, sports, music videos, game shows, documentaries. Sometimes they want to be informed, and sometimes they just want to be entertained. But they can tell the difference.

The world has a lot of television sets—about 750 million sets, or one for every six people. And people do watch a lot. In America, where most households have at least two sets, the only activity that takes up more free time is sleeping. So it's only natural that television partly shapes our lives.

Television has changed our sense of time. We take it for granted that if something big happens, we'll see it on television almost immediately. Television can literally make time go faster, with compression machines that speed up motion without distorting voices. (They are frequently used on game shows.)

"Time shifters"—people who use videocassette recorders to tape programs for later viewing—often feel frustrated when they're watching in "real time" and can't fast-forward through commercials or dull scenes. Viewers with remote control like to zap through channels, looking for something better, insisting it's possible to watch at least two programs at once.

Television has also changed our sense of space. As McLuhan predicted, it has created a global village. All over the world, viewers watch the same big events: assassinations, wars, royal weddings, Olympic Games. In fact, broadcasting tycoon Ted Turner is so sure that the world will be tuned to his Cable News Network in the event of nuclear war that he has taped a special message that will run only if the world seems to be ending. Other than the fact that it includes the hymn "Nearer My God to Thee," the message remains a secret.

But while television may unite us mentally, it drives us apart physically. In the beginning, television was hailed for bringing families together; now multiple-set homes do the opposite. Often, we watch alone. Sometimes we feel closer to people on television than to the real people around us.

Part of the lure (and danger) of television is its familiarity. "After watching family TV shows, I felt that my parents were inadequate and that I didn't have the perfect family life I saw on TV," a seventeen-year-old told a *McCall's* magazine survey. "It caused many fights and my growing apart from my family." Television families have become less "perfect" over the years. Even so, fictional problems are still solved in twenty-four or forty-eight minutes, or in a few episodes at most. Such quick solutions are rare in real life.

Television can create such a sense of intimacy that viewers develop strong feelings about people they don't know. Many "Today" fans didn't merely enjoy Jane Pauley as a host; they saw her as a friend and were angry at NBC when she left the program. Television may give us our only look at people with life-styles or problems different from our own: in San Francisco, an on-air diary called "Paul Wynne's Journal" sensitized viewers to the daily life of a real person with AIDS. This feeling of intimacy can backfire if distorted or stereotyped images are presented to us. And television is a one-way street. "I know I have a presence in people's living rooms," says Chuck Kraemer of WCVB-Channel 5, the ABC affiliate station in Boston. Kraemer is an essayist, movie reviewer, and host of the local documentary series "Chronicle." "It creates a bond, because they feel like they know me, but there's no way for me to know them."

Television can also deaden feelings. Many people avoid the news because they feel bombarded by disasters they can do nothing about, even though they know that shutting off the bad news doesn't make it end. Others watch television to relax, although studies show that people of all ages become *more* tense as they view—even if they're watching a comedy—when their minds are not being challenged. Maybe this is why we walk away and don't even bother to shut off the set. About 20 percent of the time that a television set is on, it plays to an empty room.

Within a culture, television helps define what is acceptable and what is not. On "I Love Lucy" in 1952, scriptwriters had to say that Lucy Ricardo was "expecting" because the word *pregnant* was considered in bad taste. By the 1990s a *male* character was pregnant (on "Alien Nation"), an unmarried woman gave birth to an interracial baby (on "The Days and Nights of Molly Dodd'), and a sitcom housewife often complained about premenstrual syndrome (on "Roseanne"). Some viewers blame such programs—and television in general—for warping family values. Others merely wish that most sitcoms, explicit or not, were as funny as "I Love Lucy."

The line between reality and television is often blurred, by viewers of all ages. Toddlers ask their parents to invite the latest cartoon character to their birthday parties. College students decide to become attorneys based on the unrealities of "L.A. Law." Adults send expensive gifts to characters being "married" on soap operas. The Marriott Corporation has even considered opening a chain of taverns that look like the one in "Cheers." (Will their job applicants have an edge if they look like Sam or Carla?)

Political parties have even asked television stars to run for office without asking what they stand for. That happened to news anchor Walter Cronkite in the 1970s, when he was regarded as "the most trusted man in America." But it made sense in America, where many people choose their leaders by how they appear in television debates and ads.

Television is considered essential to survival. In most states, if a person goes bankrupt, his television set cannot be seized as an asset. As a New York State law says, it is "a utensil necessary for a family," like a stove or shoes. Even homeless people try not to be cut off: in New York in 1990, people living in a shantytown chipped in to buy a television and videocassette recorder, which they plugged into a generator.

One reason that television brings so many changes is that television itself is always changing.

Equipment has brought changes. Early television was studio-bound because the typical setup of camera, lights, and sound equipment weighed over two thousand pounds. Television "opened up" as the equipment became smaller and more portable. The use of videotape and satellites revolutionized news by making it possible to broadcast almost instantly from around the world.

There are also more channels and more choices every year. The once-dominant "big three" networks—ABC, CBS, and NBC—have lost almost a third of their audience to local stations, Fox Broadcasting, pay-per-view, and dozens of cable channels. Satellite systems such as British Sky Broadcasting can broadcast directly to sets, bypassing all the old ways. With VCRs and games such as Nintendo, many sets are not used to watch real-time programs at all.

Yet with all these choices, how different is the programming from channel to channel, from year to year? Early television entertainment drew its ideas from radio and Broadway plays. Now television recycles ideas from movies, best-selling books, news items, and especially from itself. (Some of the biggest hits have been spinoffs of big hits—such as "Laverne & Shirley," one of a few series spawned from "Happy Days," and "A Different World," which descended from "The Cosby Show.") Most new shows seem so stale that fewer than half of them last for a season.

Historian Erik Barnouw tells of a network executive who pitched program ideas to sponsors by telling them that the show would be "completely new" but "exactly like" an earlier success—just as "The Simpsons" was a new idea that also recalled "The Flintstones," and "America's Funniest Home Videos" has something in common with the long-running hit "Candid Camera." Many new shows don't even pretend to be original: "The New Dragnet," "The New Lassie," "The New Adam-12," "The Munsters Today."

WWWWWWWWWWWWWW

Television isn't the only medium with the power to change people's minds and lives. Many aspects of television, good and bad, also apply to books, newspapers, radio, movies, and plays. But television reaches more people, day in and day out. It speaks to everyone because no skills are required to watch. And it's free to anyone with a set and a place to plug it in.

One of the best insights into television came from Edward R. Murrow, a journalist who was known as "the conscience of CBS." At home on radio—where stories are told in words, not pictures—Murrow nonetheless became an early television star. He said: "This instrument can teach, it can illuminate; yes, it can even inspire. But it can do so only to the extent that humans are determined to use it to those ends. Otherwise, it is merely lights and wires in a box."

THE WORLD OF TOMORROW:

Inventing Television

T elevision had a long, slow birth. It was a gleam in the eye of scientists in the late 1800s, when discoveries and inventions were tumbling forth one after another—electricity, the telephone, the phonograph, the wireless telegraph, motion pictures. The word *television* was used as early as 1900, long before sets or shows existed. But television didn't arrive "easily and cheaply" in most homes until the middle of the twentieth century.

Who invented television? It wasn't one person or even a single team. Once the telephone was invented, the idea of adding pictures

"At some time ... I hope to be able to take my inaugurations, prizefights, and football games at home. I expect to do it easily and cheaply. Only under those conditions can a television get into my home. I do not know how soon it will be, but it is the most important item of unfinished business."
—J. C. Furnas, 1936, *The First Hundred Years* (a book predicting the future)

to sound seemed natural. As early as 1879, magazines carried cartoons of viewers at home, watching sports and wars on a wall screen. Scientists on both sides of the Atlantic Ocean, and in Japan, looked for ways to make this fantasy real. To the outside world they seemed to be mad scientists or, at best, people with crazy hobbies.

The first "televisions" were primitive. Paul Nipkow, a German, and John Logie Baird, a Scot, each came up with spinning disks to transmit still pictures. The images looked like blurry shadows. A bigger problem was that the person at the receiving end also had to have a big, bulky, spinning disk to see the pictures.

Scientists tinkered with oddities like this into the 1920s. But using *electricity* to scan and transmit images was the breakthrough. In Idaho, a young man named Philo T. Farnsworth was fascinated by the possibility, perhaps because he lived on a farm without electricity until the age of fourteen. Farnsworth began experimenting while still in high school, and at the age of twenty-four he was granted the first electronic television patent. He and Vladimir Zworykin—a Russian-American who devised and patented the eye of the television camera (then called the iconoscope tube) and the television screen (then known as the kinescope picture tube)—are the fathers of modern television.

The origins of television are intertwined with the history and development of radio. Radio paved—and paid—the way for television. The television networks of NBC, CBS, and ABC all began as radio networks.

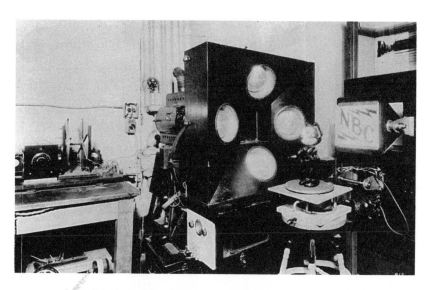

Felix the Cat was used in television testing done by NBC in 1930.
Most early television broadcasting experiments used primitive
equipment like this. AP/Wide World Photos

Radio developed from Guglielmo Marconi's wireless telegraph, invented in the late 1800s. For years radio was used
only by ships and the military. But in the 1920s it took its
place, beside phonographs and newspapers, as a source of
home entertainment and news. Putting a radio in every living
room became the goal of the Radio Corporation of America,
or RCA, which sold sets made by Westinghouse and General
Electric. These companies—along with Philco, American
Telephone & Telegraph, and others—hummed with television research. Radio had helped make them rich, and they
expected television to make them even richer.

RCA was guided by David Sarnoff, who started his career as
a Marconi telegraph operator and became world famous when
he picked up disaster signals from the ocean liner *Titanic* as
it was sinking. Sarnoff was young, smart, and persuasive. He
was a rising executive at RCA when that company created the
National Broadcasting Company, or NBC, in 1926.

Another key player was the Columbia Broadcasting
System, or CBS. Formed in 1927, it was bought a year later
by William S. Paley, who had been advertising manager of his
family's cigar company. Six months of radio ads had doubled
the firm's cigar sales, so Paley believed in the power of broadcasting. He followed NBC in creating a network of local stations across America.

Soon the airwaves were buzzing with network affiliates and
hundreds of local stations. Because they were starting to
crowd each other out, the United States government stepped
in. In 1927 Congress created the Federal Radio Commission
to oversee broadcasting. In 1934 it became the Federal
Communications Commission, or FCC.

When setting the standards for radio, the commission had television in mind. It included the transmission of *pictures* in its definition of radio—so the same rules would apply to both. The Radio Act of 1927 decreed that no one could own the airwaves; they were to be used by licensed stations "in the public interest" and paid for by ads. Anyone with a receiver could tune in for free.

Even then, some people raised questions that persist to this day. Why did television have to rely on commercials, like radio? Would too much television put America out of touch with art, science, and religion? Teachers, labor leaders, and church groups started a movement in 1933: They wanted one out of every four channels to be nonprofit—without ads. A few senators took up this cause, but it was defeated. America's broadcasting framework would be based on advertising and mass appeal. A different model took shape in Britain and other European countries, however, where most radio and television stations are owned by the government and financed by taxes instead of commercials.

The 1920s was a time for television experiments. The public didn't see them, but researchers and reporters did, on screens no bigger than the palm of a hand. In 1927 the *New York Times* marveled: FAR OFF SPEAKERS SEEN AS WELL AS HEARD HERE—LIKE A PHOTO COME TO LIFE. GE offered sets for sale to the public at seventy-five dollars. That was a lot of money then—about a month's pay for the average worker. With nothing to watch except occasional test broadcasts, only the very rich or the very curious made the investment.

Tiny local television stations sprang up here and there. Like early radio stations, these unlicensed stations were run by inventors and ham-radio operators who built their own equipment. Such stations vanished soon after the stock market crash of 1929, which led to the Great Depression of the 1930s.

The Depression plunged the United States and Europe into hard times. Even those lucky enough to work could barely scrape by. Yet entertainment thrived. Movies were cheap, radio was free, and both helped people take their minds off their troubles. The networks were still betting that someday television could be bigger than both.

In 1930 NBC opened an experimental television station, W2XBS, at RCA's new Radio City headquarters in New York. CBS followed in 1931 with its station W2XAB. Nothing was regularly scheduled: viewers got postcards from the stations telling them to watch for a dramatic play next Thursday night and perhaps a comedy on Saturday. Programs were short—half an hour or less—because the studio lights were so hot that actors wilted beneath them.

Lack of money drove W2XAB off the air by 1933, but NBC pressed on, driven by fears that Europe was beating America in the television race. In the depths of the Depression, David Sarnoff masterminded a million-dollar plan. The first step would be to *show* television to masses of people, most of whom had only heard about it. To keep them curious, NBC would offer an array of original programs, complete with a "TV mobile unit," that took cameras out of the studio and onto the streets. RCA would mass-produce sets for sale.

At this time all of NBC's television operations were based

in New York City. The company could broadcast only within fifty miles of its transmitter on the Empire State Building. So NBC's plan unfolded at the New York World's Fair in 1939, which had a fitting theme: "The World of Tomorrow."

In its pavilion at the Fair, RCA displayed not one but twelve television sets, all alive with pictures and sound. The screens were small—just five or nine inches on the diagonal—but they drew huge crowds. Viewers lined up for something new every day: puppet shows, cooking demonstrations, baseball, football, boxing, hockey, basketball, and the circus. NBC even had cameras outside the celebrity-studded New York premiere of the movie *Gone With the Wind*.

Spurred partly by NBC's success, CBS hurried back on the air. Paley's network was even ready to go one step better. It was experimenting with color television, not mere black-and-white.

But the novelty of television paled beside world events. War was raging across Europe, engineered by the dictators Adolf Hitler and Benito Mussolini. Japan had attacked China. In the United States, President Franklin D. Roosevelt declared a limited national emergency. At RCA, television soon took a backseat to a secret defense project called radar.

Americans sensed the coming of war. Television was not uppermost in their minds, although there were now twenty-three television stations across the country. The average family still couldn't spare $199.50 for RCA's lowest-priced set. World's Fair or not, only about ten thousand sets had been sold.

Then in December 1941, the United States entered World War II, and television disappeared from the air. Television couldn't cover the war; it wasn't advanced enough to broadcast across long distances, or to record live events and retransmit them. And factories had to turn out weapons, not cameras and picture tubes. Network radio continued as the chief source of news and entertainment.

Still, the war years saw some big moves in the media industry. Radio and television got a new network in 1943, when the government forced NBC to sell one of its two radio networks. That became the American Broadcasting Company, or ABC. In 1944 the television manufacturer Allen DuMont created a fourth network, which he named after himself.

The framework of the television business also took shape in those years. The national *networks*—ABC, CBS, NBC, and Du Mont—were the center of the industry. They are sometimes called *broadcast networks* or *over-the-air networks*, to differentiate them from the cable networks that came later. (After the Du Mont network left the air in the 1950s, the remaining "big three" networks didn't face national noncable competition until Fox Broadcasting was launched in the 1980s. Two other national noncable networks are Telemundo and Univision, which broadcast Spanish-language programs.)

Each over-the-air network is allowed by the FCC to own and operate a small number of stations throughout the country. Network programming is also aired by *network affiliates*, which are local stations that are paid by the network to carry a certain amount of network-supplied programs. There are about 620 network affiliates in the United States.

Many local stations are *independent*, not network-affiliated. They are owned by groups of individuals or by corporations such as Westinghouse or Metromedia. (However, to prevent monopolies, the government forbids any one person or firm to own more than seven independent stations.) There are about four hundred independent stations; most specialize in old movies, regional sports, and syndicated game and talk shows. Some are part-time affiliates of Fox Broadcasting, showing all of Fox's prime-time programs.

Cable television has its own framework, and the terms *cable network* and *cable channel* are often used interchangeably. Most cable offerings are seen nationally; everyone gets the same programs on Cable News Network (CNN), Nickelodeon, the Discovery Channel (TDC), the Weather Channel, and most other cable channels no matter where they live. Cable also has three *superstations*—WTBS-Atlanta, WOR-New York, and WGN-Chicago—which are local stations seen nationally. There are regional and local cable channels as well. Subscribers pay a monthly fee to their local *cable system* for *basic cable* service, which usually includes all over-the-air stations and many cable channels. *Premium* or *pay-cable channels*, such as HBO and Showtime, cost extra.

When World War II ended in September 1945, American television made up for lost time. Factories were geared up, returning soldiers had money to spend, and businesses were eager to advertise. Television sets began rolling off assembly lines. All picture tubes were black-and-white, because CBS had lost its battle with the government for a color television system.

The networks and many independent stations now broad-

cast for four or five nights a week. The year 1946 saw the first
regular series, the variety show "Hour Glass," and the first
soap opera, "Faraway Hill." The year 1947 brought the
opening of Congress, "Kraft Television Theater," "Howdy
Doody," "Kukla, Fran and Ollie," "Meet the Press," and
NBC's triumph: the World Series. Hundreds of forgettable
programs were also concocted just to fill time.

"Working in television then was like being in a little theater
company; everybody did everything," recalled Frances Buch,
who left radio acting for CBS television in the 1940s. Buch's
variety of assignments—a new one every few months—reflected the hodgepodge of those years. She was scorekeeper on
"CBS Television Quiz" and co-host of "Red Cross First Aid"
and "Country Dancing." Over the years Buch also served as
a director of live commercials during baseball games, the
early morning news, Bil Baird's puppet show "Whistling Wizard," and many daytime programs especially for women, including an oddity called "The Missus Goes a'Shopping,"
which highlighted the opening of new supermarkets.

"I remember with pleasure 'To the Queen's Taste,' a program of cooking lessons well before the era of Julia Child,"
Buch said. "We filmed it in the brownstone kitchen of the
chef, Dione Lucas, who tried to make use of television. Her
trademark was to stretch strudel dough and hold it up to the
camera." (Lucas would then say: "The dough should be thin
enough to read the *New York Herald Tribune* through it!")

By 1948 television was spreading across the country. Fifteen states had it; the other states were scrambling to get the
permits, transmitters, and equipment needed to begin broadcasting. Network affiliates and independent stations were

popping up so fast that the FCC had to limit licenses. In "television cities"—the metropolitan areas that were the first to have television—sets flew off store shelves, while taverns without television went broke. By now all four networks were broadcasting every night of the week.

A primitive kind of cable television began in 1948, too. Appliance dealers in hilly areas of Pennsylvania and Oregon couldn't sell televisions because reception was bad. So they put up their own big antennas on local mountaintops and ran wires to individual homes. There were no cable channels yet; most areas were lucky to have one network affiliate. But viewers happily took whatever they could get.

Anyone who doubted the power of television needed only to go out on Tuesday nights. In television cities, the streets were empty. Everyone was at home or at the local bar, watching "Mr. Television," Milton Berle.

Hoping to buy a television set for three cents, bargain hunters spent
the night outside an appliance store in New York City in May 1954.
A sign in the window said: YES! YES! 3¢! ONE ONLY EACH DAY OF SALE.
© New York Daily News, used with permission

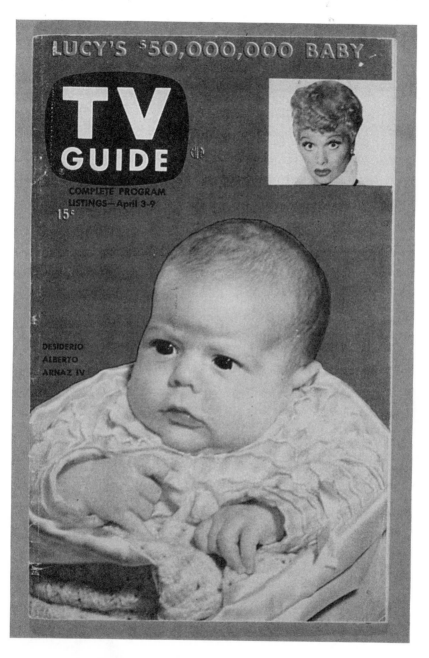

The first *TV Guide*   Reprinted with permission from TV Guide® Magazine.
© 1953 by News America Publications Inc., Radnor, Pa.

LOTS OF LAUGHS: 2

Variety and Situation Comedy

"Talent from a showerful of stars"—that was the gaudy, glittering appeal of variety shows. By the 1990s they were almost extinct. Yet the early ones and the bold ones helped put television on the map.

Variety had been popular on radio, but television brought something extra. Suddenly people could *see* what hadn't been seen since the days of vaudeville's traveling shows: comedians, singers, acrobats, dancers, jugglers, and circus acts. And they could see them close up, right at home.

Milton Berle had been a hit in vaudeville and a flop in radio. He quickly became Mr. Television, the medium's first superstar, hamming it up with skits and music on NBC's "Texaco Star Theater." Each week's introduction was sillier than the last: "And now the man with jokes from the Stone Age!" was followed by Berle bounding onto the stage dressed as a caveman. He also clowned in women's clothes. It was low-brow humor, and it helped sell television sets. When Berle debuted in 1948, only about one in fifty American households could view his antics. When he left the air eight years later, three out of four homes had sets.

CBS also introduced a hit variety show in 1948: "Toast of the Town," soon renamed "The Ed Sullivan Show," after its host. Sullivan was the opposite of Berle. He wasn't a performer. In fact, he was so awkward on stage that comedians mimicked him: "Tonight we have a reeeally big *shew!*" He also made audiences roar with introductions like these: "I'd like to prevent Robert Merrill." Sullivan had the last laugh, though. His show lasted twenty-three years.

As a show-business columnist for the *New York Daily News*, Sullivan could find and book the biggest names of the day, from singer Dinah Shore to the Bolshoi Ballet. He refused to hire blacklisted entertainers—those suspected of being Communists—but he broke early race barriers by presenting black performers. And he had a nose for rock and roll. Two acts in particular made headlines: Elvis Presley in 1956, whose "lewd" hip movements were censored by the camera; and the Beatles in 1964, whose long hair raised eyebrows across the nation.

Sid Caesar and Imogene Coca, along with sidekicks Carl Reiner and Howard Morris, created a golden age of comedy

"Mr. Television," Milton Berle, in 1951. To the delight of audiences, he often played skits in women's clothing. AP/Wide World Photos

Ed Sullivan had a "*really* big shew" the night he first invited The Beatles to appear. AP/Wide World Photos

on NBC's "Your Show of Shows." Broadcast live, this ninety-minute show had a frantic, anything-can-happen energy that has all but disappeared from television programming. Along with the standard variety acts, it featured comic genius. The show's writers were young and brilliant—among them Mel Brooks (later known for his movies *Young Franken-stein*, *Blazing Saddles*, and *Spaceballs*), Neil Simon (the playwright whose string of hits would include *The Odd Couple*, later a hit television series), Larry Gelbart (one of the creators of the television show "M*A*S*H"), and Woody Allen. The cast parodied much-loved movies: *From Here to Eternity* became *From Here to Obscurity*, and *Shane* became *Strange*. Caesar and Reiner were masters of mock interviews such as this:

> *Archaeologist* (played by Caesar): After many years
> I haff found ze secret of King Titten Totten's tomb!
> *Excited Reporter* (Reiner): What is it, Professor?
> *Archaeologist*: I should tell *you*?

"The Ernie Kovacs Show" was another landmark. Kovacs understood the visual power of television. And he was not afraid to be weird. He used trick photography to put legs on the Mona Lisa and to conjure dozens of dogs from a woman's bubble bath. Many of his skits had no words or clear endings. Television never knew quite what to do with Kovacs; he bounced from network to network before dying young. But he inspired later shows, from "Rowan & Martin's Laugh-In" to "Late Night with David Letterman."

However, most variety shows were homey and low-key, hosted by radio stars such as Arthur Godfrey, Perry Como,

Red Skelton, and Ted Mack. Audiences were less fickle then; they felt at home with the same faces, skits, and music week in and week out, and these shows survived from ten to twenty years. But by the 1970s variety seemed old, even in the hands of younger hosts like Sonny and Cher or Flip Wilson. Only "The Carol Burnett Show" endured in the old style. Programs with "something for everyone" were relics; television itself had become one big variety show.

"Rowan & Martin's Laugh-In" was in a class by itself. Launched in 1968, the show was vaudeville for the video age, with sight gags and sound bites edited into nonstop mayhem. Its silly catch phrases swept the country: "You bet your bippy," "Here come de judge," and "Look that up in your *Funk and Wagnalls.*" President Richard Nixon appeared one night to intone the most famous line, "Sock it to me." "Laugh-In" was where comedienne Lily Tomlin created her snide Ernestine the Operator (AT&T later asked her to do Ernestine commercials, but Tomlin refused) and where Arte Johnson lurked behind potted palms, dressed as a German spy who observed the chaos and called it "verrry interrresting."

Perhaps because it was slapstick, "Laugh-In" got away with poking fun at racial tensions and the Vietnam War. Tom and Dick Smothers did not; CBS canceled "The Smothers Brothers Comedy Hour" after the brothers protested that their stubborn jabs at government and religion were being censored. (Curiously, the "dumb" brother, Tom, was the creative drive behind the act—and the conscience that got them into trouble with CBS.) Their satire was replaced by the cheerfully mindless "Hee Haw," a country-music knock-off of "Laugh-In."

" 'The Waltons Eat Their Young' won't be seen tonight so that we may bring you the following live presentation." That was one of the many mock bulletins that opened "Saturday Night Live," setting the outlaw tone that the program has maintained, if unevenly, since 1975. It has launched such performers as Chevy Chase ("I'm Chevy Chase and you're not"), John Belushi, Dan Aykroyd, Gilda Radner, Jane Curtin, Bill Murray, Joe Piscopo, Eddie Murphy, Billy Crystal, Mike Myers, and Dana Carvey. It can be fresh, daring, sloppy, and dumb—often in the same night.

"SNL" set itself apart from other comedy shows by "breaking reality," as producer Lorne Michaels called it. One example was a skit in which Killer Bees buzzed into a suburban home with their Spanish-accented demand: "Your pollen or your wife, Señor." After a few minutes of similar gags, the camera drifted away from the action. The actors tried to follow the camera and keep the skit going, then Michaels strode on-screen as himself to confront the seemingly out-of-control director. Commercials for fake products such as the Bass-o-matic (a blender that could pulverize a fish, bones and all) further blurred the lines between satire and reality.

"SNL" has had its detractors, even among people who are far from straitlaced. Garry Trudeau, creator of the anti-establishment cartoon "Doonesbury," asked the 1981 graduates of Colby College to view the program more critically: "For all its innovations, this kind of satire tells society's nebbishes that they are right about themselves, that they *are* nobodies, that to be so un-hip as to be disadvantaged, to be ignorant, to be physically infirm, or black, or even female is to invite contempt."

Great or gimmicky, situation comedies have been favorites since the early days of radio. Perhaps it's because they have a comfortable, predictable pattern: a minor crisis, humorous predicaments, a neat ending, and what novelist Herbert Gold has called "happy people with happy problems." Also, most sitcoms are about families, the best-known subject of all.

Television's first sitcoms came from radio. Some were ethnic comedies, popular since the 1920s: "Amos 'n' Andy" was about black lodge brothers in Harlem, and "The Goldbergs" were a loving Jewish family from the Bronx. In later years these shows would seem stereotypical and sometimes offensive, and they would not survive in reruns.

Famous radio comedians easily made the leap to the living-room screen. "The Jack Benny Show," featuring the stingy comic who screeched away at his violin, was a long-running success. Benny's most famous radio joke played especially well on television:

> *Robber*: Your money or your life!
> *Benny* (after a long pause): I'm thinking! I'm thinking!

"The George Burns and Gracie Allen Show" also transferred well from radio. In a nod to his new surroundings, George sometimes tuned into his wife's scatter-brained antics on a television set in his study. Viewers would watch Burns himself watching his own show, then commenting on the action to the audience (a device that would pop up decades later on "Moonlighting" and "It's Garry Shandling's Show"). Each show ended with their classic sign-off:

George: Say good-night, Gracie.
Gracie: Good-night, Gracie.

Television slowly weaned itself away from radio to find its own talent. Jackie Gleason had fizzled as television's first Chester A. Riley on "The Life of Riley," but he lit up DuPont's variety showcase "Cavalcade of Stars." One of Gleason's best bits involved a loudmouthed Brooklyn bus driver with a heart of gold. The character, Ralph Kramden, made history on "The Honeymooners."

There are only thirty-nine episodes (plus a few "newly discovered" ones) of "The Honeymooners." Yet is any room on television as familiar as the shabby kitchen of Ralph and Alice Kramden? Any television sidekick as beloved as Ralph's buddy, Ed Norton? Seen in syndication worldwide, "The Honeymooners" wins new fans every day for Ralph and his universally recognizable get-rich-quick schemes.

However, the undisputed champion of television comedy is Lucille Ball, whose "I Love Lucy" first aired in 1951 and has been on reruns ever since. Viewers around the globe still roar at the escapades of Lucy, her bandleader husband, Ricky Ricardo (played by Ball's real husband, Desi Arnaz), and their neighbors Fred and Ethel Mertz. The show's premise was nothing new: a zany wife who stands up to her mock-stern husband with mischief and a few well-placed tears. But "I Love Lucy" had uncommon imagination, fine writing, and Lucille Ball. Who can forget Lucy stomping on grapes in

Italy, gulping chocolates on an assembly line, or getting locked in a walk-in freezer?

Sixty-nine percent of all viewing households were tuned into "I Love Lucy" for the birth of Little Ricky on January 19, 1953. Ball and Arnaz always had an innate sense of timing, and their real son, Desi IV, was born the same day. His arrival almost overshadowed the inauguration of President Dwight D. Eisenhower the next morning.

Hardworking dad, homemaker mom, happy kids, a house in the suburbs: that rosy picture was the model for dozens of early family sitcoms, among them "Father Knows Best," "The Adventures of Ozzie and Harriet," "Make Room for Daddy" (later called "The Danny Thomas Show"), "Leave It to Beaver," and "The Donna Reed Show." No mom around? No problem. An aunt would do, as on "The Andy Griffith Show." Or an uncle or male housekeeper could take her place, as on "My Three Sons"; viewers have always been tickled by sitcoms about men raising kids.

Problems were easy to solve in the old sitcom days. When Beaver became inquisitive and climbed into a steaming cup of "tea" on a billboard, Dad and the fire department were there to save him. When Betty on "Father Knows Best" didn't want to attend her parents' alma mater, she got to pick her own college, which just happened to be across town.

Decades later, "The Wonder Years" looked back on these innocent times with more realism. The Arnolds were a typical family, but life wasn't always ideal. The kids missed their father when he had to be away on business at Thanksgiving,

Who else could be under that urn? The world continues to love
Lucille Ball as Lucy Ricardo in "I Love Lucy." Sidekick Ethel Mertz
(played by Vivian Vance) is at right.
Wisconsin Center for Film and Theater Research

and they watched in pain as their mother ran from the dinner table in tears. They hated their dad one Christmas when he didn't buy them a color television set. Seeing his father toadying up to his boss on the golf course made thirteen-year-old Kevin Arnold cringe, but looking back on it as an adult, he finally understood why.

Idealized as they were, early family sitcoms were rooted in reality. The gimmick shows of the 1960s were gleefully unreal. Some titles told the whole story, like "My Mother the Car," "The Flying Nun," or "My Favorite Martian." Many could be summed up by their theme songs, like this one from "Mr. Ed":

> A horse is a horse, of course, of course, and no one can talk to a horse, of course. That is, of course, unless the horse is the famous Mister Ed.
>
> Go right to the source and ask the horse, he'll give you the answer that you'll endorse. He's always on a steady course. Talk to Mister Ed!
>
> People yakity-yak a streak and waste your time o'day. But Mister Ed will never speak unless he has something to say!
>
> A horse is a horse, of course, of course, and this one'll talk 'til his voice is hoarse. You never heard of a talking horse? Well, listen to this: *I am Mister Ed!*

Waves of sitcom weirdness replaced the genial shows of the past. Bizarre families popped up: "The Addams Family," "The Munsters." Women acquired the magical powers of genies ("I Dream of Jeannie") and witches ("Bewitched"). Families left the suburbs for the sticks in "Green Acres" and the sticks for the suburbs in "The Beverly Hillbillies." A comedy *about* a television show, "The Dick Van Dyke Show," finally injected some reality onto the small screen. It was as if producers and programmers were clearing the landscape for something entirely new.

CBS did an about-face in the late 1960s and early 1970s. For years its programs had appealed mainly to older, rural audiences. The shows didn't reflect what was happening in the world: upheaval over the Vietnam War, race riots, or the women's movement. And they didn't reach the young, affluent consumers that advertisers sought. CBS canceled most of its old favorites and introduced three sitcoms that revolutionized television programming. The other networks scurried to catch up.

First came "The Mary Tyler Moore Show," in 1970. Like "The Dick Van Dyke Show," it was a sitcom about television that focused more on work than family. But this time Moore, who'd been Dick Van Dyke's spouse on television, wasn't the wife. She played Mary Richards, a television news producer who was smart, attractive, and single. And unlike earlier working women in sitcoms, Mary had more than marriage on her mind. Her co-workers were her "family." They were witty, vulnerable, funny people who seemed real. When they all were fired in the final episode, viewers cried.

Several characters from "The Mary Tyler Moore Show" went on to series of their own: "Rhoda," "Phyllis," and "Lou Grant." This spinoff trend helped make television seem even more real; now viewers could watch their favorite characters grow and change. After the Mary Tyler Moore "family'" had set the standard, some of the best sitcoms were set in the workplace, from "Taxi" and "Cheers" to "The Bob Newhart Show" and "Murphy Brown."

CBS's next big move came in 1971, when "All in the Family" jolted television to a new level of reality. The lead character, Archie Bunker, was a blue-collar worker not unlike Ralph Kramden of "The Honeymooners." But Archie hated all minorities and called them names never before heard on the air. He gleefully defended his views to his patient wife, their daughter and "egghead liberal" son-in-law, his black neighbors, and anyone who would listen. No issue was taboo. Along with race, "All in the Family" tackled impotence, menopause, homosexuality, rape, abortion, the Vietnam War, welfare, and U.S. foreign policy. This exchange was typical:

> *Gloria* (Archie's daughter): You can't even bear the mention of the word "sex."
> *Archie*: I don't allow no four-letter words in my house!

The program had its critics. Some hated Carroll O'Connor's portrayal of Archie as a "lovable" bigot. Others took offense at the language and subject matter. A few even complained that the show was tamer than the British series that inspired it, "Till Death Do Us Part." But viewers lapped it up for years and faithfully followed its characters in the spinoffs "Archie Bunker's Place," "The Jeffersons," "Maude," and "Good Times."

While "All in the Family" changed what could be said on television, "M*A*S*H" blurred the lines between comedy and drama. Certainly the setting was unfunny—a Mobile Army Surgical Hospital unit in the thick of the Korean War. The

Jean Stapleton and Carroll O'Connor as Edith and Archie Bunker on
"All in the Family," one of the 1970s sitcoms that changed the face
of television. Wisconsin Center for Film and Theater Research

characters relied on humor to survive red tape, daily despair, and senseless death.

Turning a movie into a weekly television series is rarely successful, but M*A*S*H was an exception. It debuted on television in 1972, when the Vietnam War had been raging for years. Audiences were ready for the show's dark, antiwar humor. The final episode, a movie-length farewell in which the war ended, aired in 1983 and by 1991 was still the most-watched program of all time (excluding the Super Bowl). In "M*A*S*H" style, it was not a happily ever-after finale. Alan Alda's character, Hawkeye, collapsed in a nervous breakdown. Major Winchester, a culture snob, enjoyed a classical concert at last—then saw the musicians senselessly killed.

Sitcoms as grim as "M*A*S*H" all but disappeared in the 1980s. Certainly the hit comedy of that decade, "The Cosby Show," was closer in spirit to "Father Knows Best" and other family sitcoms of the 1950s and 1960s. An affluent, affectionate black family was a television breakthrough, and people of all ages loved watching the Huxtable kids grow up. Yet some viewers felt the show "didn't relate to the harsher realities of many black people," as critic John J. O'Connor wrote in the *New York Times*. "It's all very encouraging, and far too easy."

A new trend balanced "The Cosby Show": blue-collar, in-your-face sitcoms with a jaded view of family life. *TV Guide*'s Harold Polskin dubbed them shows about OINKS: One Insufficient Income with Nasty Kids and Spouse. "Roseanne" led the pack. Roseanne Conner was the first sitcom mom to come home from a hard day at the beauty salon and dream

"The Cosby Show" was the most-watched series of the 1980s. Bill Cosby created it partly because he was tired of situation comedies in which "the children were brighter than the parents." It was also the first sitcom to portray African Americans as established professionals. AP/Wide World Photos

THE SIMPSONS

"The Simpsons," those animated upstarts, carved out their own
niche in prime time. "The Simpsons"™
© 1991 Twentieth Century Fox Film Corporation. Used with permission

about killing her husband and kids when they banged on the bathroom door. The Bundy family of "Married . . . with Children" made life at the Conner household look neat and serene. Compared to both, the usual sitcoms about divorce, remarriage, and stepfamilies seemed calm.

Perhaps reality is easier to take in cartoon form. "The Simpsons" may have featured the ultimate jaded television family. Homer and Marge bickered; Bart talked back to everyone except the bigger kids who bullied him. (Once a proud underachiever, he changed a bit after almost being left back in the fourth grade: "Okay, I'm as dumb as a post. Think I'm happy about it?") Brainy sister Lisa was sometimes annoyingly good.

In one memorable episode, Bart and Lisa squared off at opposite ends of the living room with their baby sister between them. They asked Maggie to "come to the one who loves you best." Sucking her pacifier, Maggie looked back and forth at her siblings. Finally she crawled toward the television set and embraced it. That may be the best comment yet on television, families, and sitcoms.

SOMETIMES SERIOUS: 3

Drama, Action/Adventure, Docudrama, TV Movies

Police officers, detectives, spies. Doctors, lawyers, judges. Newspaper reporters, cowboys, space travelers. And, for good measure, a few plain old moms, dads, and kids. These are the good guys, who fight the bad guys, who together make up the world of television drama.

Drama was different in the first days of television, remembered as the Golden Age. Practically every night the networks presented serious plays by serious playwrights— the kind of programming now found mainly on PBS, Arts and Entertainment, or Home Box Office. Several thousand original dramas were aired during the 1950s.

"The main thing was, we took ourselves seriously. We sat down and said 'I'm going to write something *good.*'"
—J. P. Miller, author of *Days of Wine and Roses* and other television plays of the 1950s

"Everything on TV is a cop show. It just is."
—Steven Bochco, creator or co-creator of "Hill Street Blues," "L.A. Law," "Doogie Howser, M.D.," "Cop Rock," and "The Bold Ones"

Television began in New York City, so it drew heavily on Broadway actors and writers. Also, plays were easier to broadcast than other types of dramas. Videotape and hand-held cameras didn't exist, so scenes couldn't be shot outdoors. Action had to take place in a studio, on one stage, where it could be captured by bulky television cameras.

Like early comedies and variety shows, television dramas of the late 1940s and early 1950s were performed live. They carried a sense of excitement and urgency, as well as the chance for colossal failure. If an actor flubbed a line or if scenery crashed to the floor, viewers saw and heard it. Nothing could be done over. Each performance was like an opening night.

Because they took place within three walls, television plays were packed with emotion rather than action. Most were good, some were as overwrought as soap operas, and a few were masterpieces. No one who has seen *Marty*, written by Paddy Chayefsky for "Goodyear TV Playhouse" in 1953, can forget the main character's cry when his mother urges him to socialize and look for a wife: "I don't want to get hurt no more! I don't want to go to the Waverly Ballroom! I had enough pain. No thank you. I'm gonna stay home and watch Sid Caesar. I'm a fat little man! A fat ugly little man!"

The Golden Age launched the careers of actors such as Jack Lemmon and Robert Redford. Great movies such as *Twelve Angry Men* were adopted from its dramas. But its main legacy has been to show how powerful television can be. Then and now, the ingredients are the same: honest words and emotions, good performers, programmers who take risks, and viewers who want the best.

New York City, 1957: A stage set from the Golden Age of Television. CBS used it for dramas and quiz shows. Bess Myerson, a former Miss America, is at right. © New York Daily News, used with permission

Television drama changed radically when lighter cameras made it possible to escape the confines of the studio. And televised movies helped to make live drama extinct.

Film producers had seen television as an enemy until the mid-1950s, when they realized there was money to be made by selling movies to the small screen. Local stations that had been producing their own programs soon found it much cheaper to run old films, sometimes around the clock. In New York, for example, WOR-TV went from presenting live drama every night of the week to recycling the same film night and day as that week's "Million Dollar Movie." Film studios such as Disney and Warner began to produce for television, and Hollywood became America's television capital.

By 1959 television drama had galloped onto the movie-set frontiers of the Old West. Thirty cowboys series had replaced Golden Age dramas, with shoot-'em-ups like "Cheyenne," "Maverick," "The Rifleman," "Bat Masterson," "Rawhide," and "Death Valley Days" lasting well into the 1960s.

As television historian Jeff Greenfield has noted, the only way to tell most Westerns apart was by the type of gun the hero carried. Some were exceptions, of course. "Gunsmoke" was the granddaddy of Westerns; it began on radio in 1952 and ran on television for twenty years, beginning in 1955. Its characters were more like real people than the cardboard figures on most other Westerns. "Bonanza," America's top-rated Western for thirteen years, had a novel gimmick. A cowboy father and his three sons ran a cattle empire, and there were rarely any women around.

Why were Westerns so popular for so long? In part they reflected the Cold War mood of the times, when America and the Soviet Union were wary of each other. Westerns, after all, were—and still are—always about heroes and villains. They delivered action-packed entertainment to a fast-growing audience. As long as viewers kept watching, producers kept producing Westerns.

But by the 1970s, programs about cops and lawyers had replaced cowboy dramas. City streets and courtrooms offered a more complicated sense of right and wrong. And viewers who thirsted for violence could find it almost anywhere on the dial. But television genres run in cycles, and now Western fans can find plenty of reruns (and even an occasional new series) on the Cowboy TV Network and other cable channels.

Police, detectives, and spies are among television's sturdiest citizens. They claimed their turf early with "Dragnet," a radio holdover and one of the first television series that was filmed rather than broadcast live. Based on cases from the Los Angeles Police Department files, it is still remembered for Sergeant Joe Friday's famous request: "Just the facts, ma'am." "The Untouchables" depicted the gangster-ridden Chicago of the 1920s and 1930s. For the sheer number of shoot-outs and deaths, it may hold the record as television's most violent show.

Like television cowboys, crime fighters are basically alike—except on the surface. Cannon was fat, Columbo was sloppy, Longstreet was blind. "I Spy" presented television's first interracial team. Ironside worked from a wheelchair. Tough

On "Bonanza," as on most westerns, the good guys always wore
white hats. Surrounding the fallen man are series patriarch Ben
Cartwright and sons Hoss and Little Joe (Lorne Greene, Dan
Blocker, and Michael Landon—left to right in foreground).
Wisconsin Center for Film and Theater Research

man Kojak sucked lollipops. The Six Million Dollar Man looked normal but boasted "bionic strength." Magnum, P.I., was sexy. Charlie's Angels were cute. Jessica Fletcher of "Murder, She Wrote" wasn't a detective at all but a widowed mystery writer with a sweet nature and a razor-sharp mind.

One 1980s show, "Cagney & Lacey," reflected the changes happening in television drama as well as comedy. The lead characters were women police detectives who were partners with very different lives. Cagney was single and well-off, while Lacey was a blue-collar wife and mother with money problems. The series looked at their frictions and friendship on and off the job. "Cagney & Lacey" had its share of gunfire, but it was really about relationships.

"Hill Street Blues" was another police landmark. It was gritty and intense, with plots and conversations spilling over each other. Scenes moved fast and episodes didn't end neatly. The top good guy, Captain Furillo, was a recovering alcoholic, and it wasn't always clear who the bad guys were. The "Hill Street" language was rawer than any heard on television to that point; one of the milder lines was Detective Belker's question to a criminal: "Would you like to sit down, hairball, or would you prefer internal bleeding?" Creator Steven Bochco had fought NBC for these liberties, and he won.

Many "Hill Street" innovations weren't entirely new. "Naked City" (a hard-nosed drama that debuted in 1958) and "Barney Miller" (an offbeat police sitcom that ran from 1975 to 1982) had been, respectively, shocking and funny. Bochco also drew direct inspiration from "The Police Tapes," a PBS documentary. But "Hill Street Blues" dared to be outrageous, week after week. It took a while to catch on; some viewers found it too confusing. Yet it soon set a new standard. Overlapping, ongoing stories became more plentiful, and television drama grew less tame.

In the 1980s, "Miami Vice" and "Moonlighting" also made waves. Executives at NBC wanted a series that could be described as "MTV cops," and certainly "Miami Vice" had a sleek, music-video look. Critics, however, called it an old-fashioned police show in a new package. "Moonlighting," on ABC, was the opposite. Set in an outlandish detective agency, it never took itself seriously. Series creator Glenn Gordon Caron admitted he was bored with television and said his characters were, too. Most episodes opened with one of the partners—elegant Maddie or smart-mouthed David—commenting on what would happen. (Unfortunately, these wink-at-the-camera segments have been edited out of some reruns to make room for extra commercials.) When Maddie needed counseling, she called Dr. Joyce Brothers. When David did, he called the singer Ray Charles. When Maddie and David's on-and-off romance finally took hold, the show felt too normal.

As the networks fought to keep viewers in the 1990s, they took a few more risks. Steven Bochco bombed with "Cop Rock," television's first musical drama. "Twin Peaks" was a bizarre soap opera/mystery that, on the surface, investigated the murder of teenager Laura Palmer. But logic was beside the point. (As Bobby Briggs said to Sheriff Truman: "You think that because I wasn't at football practice I killed my girlfriend?") "Twin Peaks" was mostly about images, concocted by creators David Lynch and Mark Frost: an FBI agent who loved his pie, a fish found in a coffeepot, a lady who spoke to her log.

Many attorneys never set foot inside a courtroom, although one would never know it from watching television. Guilt and innocence are powerful subjects, and trial lawyers have always played a role on the small screen.

"Perry Mason," a long-running series based on books by Erle Stanley Gardner, featured a lawyer who was slightly larger than life. In his first nine years, Mason lost only one case. (When asked about this by a fan, actor Raymond Burr supposedly said: "Madam, you only see the cases I try on Saturday.") "The Defenders," created by Golden Age writer Reginald Rose, was more realistic. It discussed censorship, military crime, and even abortion—before that practice was legal in the United States or even mentioned in public. In an Emmy-winning episode, it also dared to take the television industry to task for blacklisting actors and directors during the 1950s.

In the 1980s and 1990s, "L.A. Law" redefined legal drama. Its writers relished social issues with a cruel or bizarre side, like dwarf-tossing or the rights of brain-damaged boxers. Many real lawyers enjoyed the program but felt it falsely glamorized their profession.

Like television lawyers, TV doctors and nurses are stock characters who grapple with issues of life and death. The popular healers of the 1960s, Ben Casey and Dr. Kildare, from the shows of the same names, were young and idealistic—but not as young as "Doogie Howser, M.D.," the teenage

"L.A. Law" wasn't all legal drama. In this episode, uptight attorney Douglas Brackman, Jr. (played by Alan Rachins), won a spot on "Wheel of Fortune." Vanna White played herself.   AP/Wide World Photos

genius who came almost thirty years later. In their own way, all three were as unrealistic as "Marcus Welby, M.D.," which glorified the era of wise, kindly family doctors who made house calls. It was fitting that Dr. Welby was played by Robert Young, who had endeared himself to a generation of viewers as the wise, kindly dad in "Father Knows Best."

Medical shows plunged into realism with "St. Elsewhere," about a Boston public hospital beset by crises. One episode made a brilliant comment on medical costs by silently displaying the charges for one patient's treatment in the corner of the screen. (Two aspirin cost twelve dollars.) Like many dramas of the 1980s, "St. Elsewhere" got weirder (and less popular) each year. The last episode "revealed" that the entire series had been the fantasy of the chief doctor's autistic son: The little boy sat transfixed by a snow globe with a model of the hospital inside.

Newsrooms aren't as crisis-prone as medical wards, but journalists who report good stories also make good stories. "Lou Grant," a spinoff of "The Mary Tyler Moore Show," said more than most programs about the relationships of people at work. Lou, a hard-nosed city editor, hated to see his boss kowtow to the owner of the fictional *Los Angeles Tribune*, the equally hard-nosed Mrs. Pynchon. Then Lou himself would butt heads with her and lose. From time to time, "Lou Grant" also tackled an issue that upsets journalists and the public alike: the question of whether or not reporters should leave crime victims and their families in peace.

〰〰〰〰〰〰〰〰

Science fiction is a small but influential part of TV drama. The most brilliant example is "The Twilight Zone," which took place in that "middle ground between light and shadow, between science and superstition." The series blended horror and wit in a new tale each week. It was created, hosted, and often written by Rod Serling, a giant of the Golden Age. One of the classic episodes was titled "Escape Clause," about a man who sells his soul to the devil in exchange for eternal life. He then commits murder, expecting to be sentenced to death and believing that he cannot die. The scheme backfires when he gets a life sentence—and lives forever, in prison.

"Star Trek," television's most famous space fantasy, does seem immortal. When it debuted in the mid-1960s, shows like "Iron Horse" and "Mr. Terrific" beat it in the ratings. But "Star Trek" has since fueled fan clubs, conventions, movies, books, magazines, parodies, endless worldwide reruns, and a television sequel. Some Trekkies say the best original episode was "Space Seed," in which a scientifically engineered "perfect man" emerges from suspended animation and fights for control of the starship *Enterprise*. Others champion "The Trouble with Tribbles," about fuzzy creatures that threaten the food supply of the *Enterprise* crew and their enemies. "Star Trek" is so firmly fixed in American culture that a model of the starship *Enterprise* hangs in the Smithsonian Institution in Washington, D.C.

Yet science fiction on television is tricky. A new "Twilight Zone," created in the 1980s, never quite captured the eeriness of the old one—while HBO's "Tales from the Crypt" has sometimes been even scarier. Steven Spielberg, who struck gold on film with *Star Wars*, flopped on television with

"Amazing Stories." Fantasy is even trickier. "Beauty and the Beast," featuring a sewer-dwelling monster who quoted Shakespeare, enchanted its fans but could not win a big network audience. After pressure from impassioned viewers, it found a new home on the Family Channel.

Is there room in television drama for people who don't battle the big issues of life and death, good and evil, right and wrong? The answer seems to be yes, but not much room. Ordinary people and families are more at home on situation comedies, with some major exceptions.

Many of television's most durable families have been old-fashioned ones: the nineteenth-century pioneers of "Little House on the Prairie," or "The Waltons," an Appalachian clan that stayed together through the Great Depression of the 1930s. To contrast these nostalgic tales there was the 1970s clan in "Family." They had everything the Waltons didn't: divorce, terminal illness, alcoholism, and kids who ran away from home.

In the 1980s "thirtysomething" held a mirror to the segment of the baby-boom generation that was just starting to have babies of its own. For some viewers, the characters were too self-absorbed and privileged. But many people in their thirties saw their concerns up there on the screen: how weird it felt to be a boss, how miserable it was to have to fire someone, how scary it was when you couldn't find a baby-sitter you trusted. And "thirtysomething" cut to the bone when it dealt with cancer as an ongoing story line.

In the 1990s the Thatchers of "Life Goes On" were the

most "typical" middle-class family on dramatic television. Yet they had challenges: son Corky had Down's syndrome. So did the actor (Chris Burke) who played him. This piece of casting was a first for television, and it opened viewers' eyes to the potential of those with Down's syndrome.

When a family pops up in a made-for-TV movie, it's a good bet that they are in trouble. Some skeptics call these "crisis-of-the-week" or "disease-of-the-month" movies. But this is how prime-time television talks about touchy issues, and some of the dramas have been critically acclaimed: "Something about Amelia" (about incest), "That Certain Summer" (homosexuality), and "An Early Frost" (AIDS).

Drama is what makes fact-based stories and historical miniseries so powerful. It adds flesh-and-blood feelings to mere facts. It also raises questions of accuracy: How much of what is shown really happened, and how much is left out? Did the actual people say and do what is shown on screen? And in the case of docudramas about events that might happen in the future—such as nuclear doomsday ("The Day After") or Soviet invasion ("Amerika")—does sensationalism begin to take over?

David Wolper, who produced the phenomenal miniseries "Roots," insists such programs can't and shouldn't take the place of newspapers and history books. They are entertainment. "What we do is create dialogue to give you a sense of what went on at that time. . . . [A docudrama] is not a reference book," Wolper has said.

And sometimes there is a larger dramatic truth.

Made-for-TV movies about fatal diseases reached new heights with
the award–winning "Brian's Song" (1971). It depicted the true
friendship between Chicago Bears teammates Gale Sayers (played
by Billy Dee Williams, pictured at right) and Brian Piccolo (James
Caan), who died of cancer at age 26.

"Holocaust" depicted Hitler's extermination of the Jews during World War II through the eyes of a Jewish family. When it aired in Germany, it helped many non-Jewish Germans face feelings of guilt. They telephoned the network by the thousands, says German producer Peter Marthesheimer, "to make personal confessions."

Speaking in the 1988 PBS documentary "Television," Marthesheimer summarized why television drama can be so powerful. "I had seen a lot of [Holocaust] programs on German TV that had been made with more accuracy, with more brains, with more delicacy. But this was the first time I was moved in my stomach. Other times I was moved in my head. You don't look from the outside at other people going in the gas chamber. *You* go, for yourself. I think this is the secret of Hollywood productions."

NIGHT AND DAY:

Daytime Programs, Soap Operas, Game Shows, Talk Shows

t NBC in the 1950s, there was a debate: Children might enjoy cartoons early in the morning, but weren't adults too busy to watch television then?

NBC decided to find out. "Today" began in 1952 with these words from host Dave Garroway: "If it doesn't sound too revolutionary, I really believe it begins a new kind of TV."

"Today" didn't really catch on until Garroway was joined in 1953 by a curious co-host, the chimpanzee J. Fred Muggs. It was feared the show was too verbal, and Muggs definitely added visual interest. "Today" went on to fill more hours

"The idea of a nation of housewives sitting mute before the video machine when they should be tidying up the premises or preparing the formula is not something to be grasped hurriedly. Obviously it is a matter fraught with peril of the darkest sort."
—Jack Gould, television critic for the *New York Times* (1952)

"People will say to 20 million people [on television] what they won't say in their dining rooms."
—Oprah Winfrey, talk-show host, actress, and producer (1989)

On the fifth anniversary of "Today," in 1957, chimpanzee J. Fred Muggs took over the cake-cutting duties from anchor Dave Garroway.   AP/Wide World Photos

than any other show on television, and it became a training ground and showcase for notables such as Hugh Downs, Barbara Walters, Edwin Newman, John Chancellor, Frank McGee, Joe Garagiola, Tom Brokaw, Gene Shalit, Jane Pauley, and Bryant Gumbel. It proved that millions of Americans *would* start their day in front of the television set.

Dozens of morning programs on the national and local level offer what "Today" does: an easy-to-digest buffet of news, conversation, interviews, traffic reports, and forecasts from a jolly weather person. But "Today" was the first and, for decades, the most popular. In the late 1980s ABC's "Good Morning America" surged ahead, partly by focusing less on news and more on entertainment. "Today" lost even more ground when Jane Pauley left the show. "The Beloved One," as Pauley's husband, Garry Trudeau, jokingly called her, was seen as a wronged woman when the younger, blonder Deborah Norville joined the show and eventually replaced Pauley. Loyal viewers felt as if their family were being torn apart, and many abandoned "Today" when Pauley did. Ironically, Norville soon left the show and was replaced by the more popular Katherine Couric—a sequence of moves that illustrated the importance of "chemistry" between viewers and hosts.

Contestants squeal, clocks count down the precious seconds, and viewers play along with their favorite television game shows—morning, afternoon, and evening.

Game shows with celebrity panels have always been popular, from the early quiz shows on radio to television favorites

Behind the game board of "Tic Tac Dough." This 1950s game show
was revived in the 1980s. © New York Daily News, used with permission

like "To Tell the Truth" and "Hollywood Squares." But many viewers prefer it when the contestants are ordinary people. It doesn't even seem to matter when the contestants are encouraged to make fools of themselves, as on the old "Beat the Clock" or the long-running "The Dating Game" or "Family Feud." (Perhaps this is because almost everyone secretly wants to be on a game show—not necessarily to win, but simply to take part.)

During the late 1950s, however, game shows *were* about winning. Big money was involved on "21," "Dotto," "The $64,000 Question," and other prime-time quizzes. Winners returned week after week, piling up huge cash awards. Some became instant "stars." One "21" contestant, Charles Van Doren, made the cover of *Time* and won a contract on "Today." Even the losers fared well, earning consolation prizes such as expensive cars.

At the height of the frenzy, the airwaves were filled with eight prime-time quiz shows that drew almost 90 percent of the viewing audience. By 1955, "The $64,000 Question" was so popular that it outranked "I Love Lucy." Indeed, when sponsor Revlon advertised a certain lipstick on that program, stores sold out of it the next day.

To keep up the momentum, some game-show producers drew on ad revenues to quadruple their prizes. But the stakes couldn't continue to rise. Scandals were uncovered, and game shows were changed forever.

Almost since the big-money quizzes began, rumors had circulated that some shows were rigged. The truth came out in 1958, when a grand jury found that contestants on "21" and "Tic Tac Dough" had been given answers in advance. As

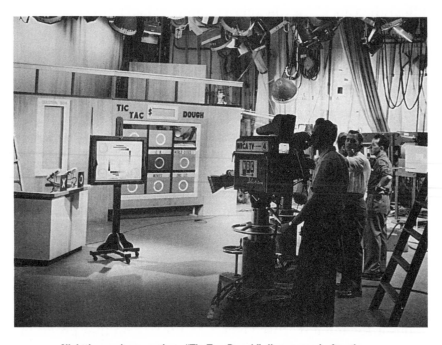

Nighttime quizzes such as "Tic Tac Dough" disappeared after the quiz-show scandal. Audiences were horrified to learn that many of these shows were rigged. © New York Daily News, used with permission

Charles Van Doren testified, "I was deeply involved in deception." Albert Freedman, producer of "21," saw the fakery as a variation on a common practice. In his eyes, it wasn't much different from a presidential speech written by a ghost writer. The industry seemed to feel that quizzes were meant to be entertaining, not necessarily honest.

But America was shocked. Congressional hearings began, and even President Dwight D. Eisenhower spoke out on the scandal. The networks quickly canceled all prime-time game shows and formed standards and practices departments to avoid future fraud. Since that time it has been a felony to rig a game show.

Oddly, the scandal inspired one of the most popular game shows ever. Merv Griffin, a former game-show host, wondered what would happen if contestants were given answers—but had to supply the questions. The result was "Jeopardy!" which began in a morning slot in the 1960s. "Jeopardy!" had timeless appeal.

As a game-show creator, Griffin also hit the jackpot in the 1980s with "Wheel of Fortune," which grew out of the pencil-and-paper game of "hangman" he played as a boy on auto trips. Aired twice daily in the United States, the game is also a hit in forty other countries. In its evening slot, it often wins more viewers than the nightly news. Some people credit the show's success to Vanna White, the smiling woman who turns the letters and waves good-bye. Yet viewers who couldn't care less about her still enjoy solving the puzzles. "Wheel" is so popular, and game shows are so cheap to produce, that they may even return to prime-time network television.

Cable has added some good new twists to the genre. Young

people have their own game shows on Nickelodeon: "Double Dare" is like a giant food fight (the show employs fifteen workers to clean up after each episode), and "What Would You Do?" asks participants how they would react in odd situations—such as being waited on by a salesman whose toupee is falling off. MTV's "Remote Control," in which couch-potato contestants answer questions about TV trivia, has drawn more viewers than the network's music videos. Its success inspired the network to look into producing talk shows and soaps as well. As Doug Herzog, senior vice president of MTV, told *Newsweek*: "Rock and roll isn't just long hair and guitars. It's irreverent. That's why 'Remote Control' fits so perfectly."

Like many another type of television, soap operas came straight from radio. Even the nickname carried over: "soap" for the detergent makers who sponsored the programs, "opera" for the melodramatic plots. The television industry prefers to call them "daytime serials."

Television's first soaps, "Search for Tomorrow" and "Love of Life," began in 1951. "Guiding Light," which debuted on radio in 1937, arrived on TV in 1952 and is still going strong in the 1990s. Like all daytime serials they became more explicit over the years, but many things about soap operas never really change.

Life is never humdrum on the soaps. The characters are always dramatic, their lives full of glamour and suffering. There is no end to their marital woes, illnesses, addictions, lawsuits, and other crises. ("Santa Barbara" resorted to a serial murder and an earthquake to kill off a glut of characters.)

Fans often act as if daytime characters are real. Constance Ford of "Another World" has told of leaving the women's room during intermission at a Broadway play when a woman stopped her with plot advice: "Listen, do something about your granddaughter Amanda—that kid's gone off the tracks!" (More patient than many actors in similar situations, Ford discussed the show with the fan for fifteen minutes.)

Soap operas have often embraced subjects considered taboo on prime time. In 1987 "Another World" introduced a character with AIDS. In 1988 daytime television got its first male homosexual character: Hank Eliot on "As the World Turns." And while characters on other dramas may mention plastic surgery, only a soap opera has shown it. In 1984 actress Jeanne Cooper, playing Kay Chancellor, allowed footage of her own facelift to air on CBS's "The Young and the Restless."

Why do soap operas endure? Partly it's the satisfaction of following a story, loving or hating the players, and keeping up with the changes. (More than one fan of Susan Lucci's on "All My Children" can recite her character's entire name: Erica Kane Martin Brent Cudahy Chandler Montgomery Montgomery. She married Montgomery twice, and new last names are always possible!) Some experts say that soap operas help viewers learn how to handle their own personal problems. Others say that the programs add excitement to lives that are otherwise dull.

Soaps are complicated, and this makes for loyalty, too. Learning all the characters and subplots is like being initiated

Susan Lucci, supported by eight of the men who have wooed her character Erica Kane on "All My Children."   AP/Wide World Photos

into a club. In fact, Jeanne Cooper tried to channel her fans' energy into social good by founding the Katherine Chancellor Society. Members contribute to the betterment of society by volunteering at a charity or substance-abuse program, and many have reported back on their good deeds.

Soap-opera audiences are among the most devoted television watchers. And it's not just women who tune in. The programs draw fan mail from adult men and students of both sexes in high school and college. Nor must viewers be at home during the day: VCRs have helped keep soaps alive.

Soaps are so popular that they have inevitably drawn parodies, such as "Soap" and "Mary Hartman, Mary Hartman." They have also inspired some of the juiciest hour-long dramas in prime time, featuring characters who scheme and love with wicked abandon. The genre began in the 1960s with "Peyton Place," then exploded in the late 1970s with "Dallas." Starring Larry Hagman as smiling schemer J. R. Ewing, "Dallas" closed its 1980 season with the cliffhanger that tantalized the world: who shot J. R.? Gambling parlors took bets on the question all summer and fall. Security on the set was so tight that even the actors didn't know the answer, because they had filmed several possible endings. The opening episode, in November, was a record-breaker: almost eight of every ten viewers tuned in. (The culprit was J. R.'s sister-in-law and mistress, Kristin Shepard.)

"Dallas" inspired "Dynasty," "Falcon Crest," "Knots Landing," and a crop of other prime-time soaps. These programs have been among America's most popular television exports, especially in Europe and South America, where viewers can't seem to get enough of the shows' slick melodrama.

wwwwwwwwwww

Daytime serials turn personal and social problems into drama. Daytime discussion shows give them to us straight. They have all but replaced the game shows and bland talk shows that once prevailed between 3:00 P.M. and 5:00 P.M. In each, the host listens, asks questions, and walks among the live studio audience—mostly women—for questions and comments.

The earliest host of the genre was Phil Donahue. His guests have poured out their experiences in everything from class reunions to wives-in-law ("She married him first—*she* married him next!"). Donahue is amiable and sometimes too eager to enter into the spirit of the subject—as when he donned a skirt to prove a point about cross-dressing.

Those who seek a steadier diet of daytime sensationalism have found it on "Geraldo," where host Geraldo Rivera doesn't shy away from provocation. In a memorable program titled "Teen Hatemongers," a brawl broke out between white supremacists and black civil-rights activist Roy Innis. The audience stormed the stage, and Rivera's nose was broken by a flying chair. He wore his bandages proudly for weeks. It was a high—or low—moment for the genre that some have dubbed "tabloid TV."

For a woman's slant in this time slot, the main choice has been Oprah Winfrey. She focuses on such topics as "People Who Were Humiliated in Childhood" or "How Divorce Affects Friends of the Couple" with warmth and earthy humor. Also a talented actress, producer, and businesswoman, Winfrey has the quintessential television personality. When

Oprah Winfrey is among television's most successful personalities, both on screen and behind the scenes.

people watch her, they feel she is talking to them as a friend. Winfrey herself sometimes provides the subject for her show. Hers is a rags-to-riches story: she overcame childhood poverty and abuse to find wealth and success. Winfrey's studio audience screamed with delight when she strode on stage in size-ten jeans pulling a little red wagon containing sixty-seven pounds of animal fat. That was the amount of weight she'd lost in one year, and fans had rooted for her as she'd shed each ounce. The fact that Winfrey gained some of it back and proclaimed, "No more diets!" only made her seem more "real."

It's an industry slogan that everyone has two businesses: his own business and show business. That may be why late-night talk shows never seem to die: they put celebrities into our homes.

The first such shows, "Chesterfield Supper Club" and "Broadway Open House," let viewers eavesdrop as the smart set gathered after the theater or an evening on the town. Steve Allen followed this format as the host of "Tonight," a live broadcast that began on NBC's local New York station in 1953. It was picked up by NBC's national network in 1954 as "The Tonight Show." Allen's replacement host was Ernie Kovacs, the outrageous comic who soon left for his own comedy-variety hour.

For five years "The Tonight Show" was "The Jack Paar Show," renamed for the host, who was smart, cranky, and given to emotional outbursts. Once, feeling he was unfairly censored, Paar walked off the set in tears. People watched him in fascination and occasional discomfort.

To replace Paar in 1962, NBC took a chance on a young comedian best known for his work as a host in game shows, Johnny Carson. He was not the network's first choice; the job had been turned down by Bob Newhart, Jackie Gleason, Joey Bishop, and Groucho Marx. Carson did *not* have the classic television personality—he wasn't hearty and warm. (However, his sidekick, Ed McMahon, was.) But Carson was funny, calm, and predictable, in many ways the opposite of Paar. He became the king of late-night television.

Joan Rivers, who had frequently guest-hosted for Carson, couldn't challenge his reign with her own late-night show. (People even tuned into Carson just to hear him mock her efforts.) Other failed challengers were Dick Cavett, whose talk shows tended to be serious rather than light, Pat Sajak of "Wheel of Fortune," and comedian Alan Thicke. Only the Fox Network's Arsenio Hall prospered against Carson. Of course, Hall appeals to a younger audience—but so does Jay Leno, the popular guest host who succeeded Carson in 1992.

As Carson and Leno came to "own" the 11:30 P.M. talk-show slot, so 12:30 A.M. was captured by David Letterman, who learned some tricks of the trade as a guest host for Carson. "Late Night with David Letterman," where hip guests let their hair down and pets do silly tricks, has become a fixture.

From a business standpoint, talk shows prove the old saying, "Talk is cheap": their production costs are low. "The pendulum is swinging back," says Fred Silverman, the producer who has programmed for the "big three" networks. "A lot of television is radio, with pictures."

MAY THE BEST IMAGE WIN:

5

News and Politics

Insiders have a saying that sums up the strength and weakness of television news: "No pictures, no story."

This relentless drive for "pictures"—meaning film or video footage with strong visual impact—is a far cry from the days when news telecasts were essentially radio bulletins with a camera. Pioneer news anchors Douglas Edwards (CBS) and John Cameron Swayze (NBC) did their jobs using little more than words. There were no reports from the field; the only visuals were occasional photographs or movie newsreel clips. Sometimes, just to create a little movement, Edwards or Swayze would get up and sit on his desk instead of sitting behind it.

Then as now, however, viewers picked their news source by whether they "liked" the people on screen. As with entertainers, they gravitated toward TV newscasters they trusted or knew from radio. They chose the people they wanted in their homes.

Political parties were quick to sense the power of television. Both the Republicans and Democrats held their 1948 presidential conventions in Philadelphia, which allowed them to televise to fourteen stations on the East Coast. This was seen by many as an exercise in democracy, however, not a spectacle to dazzle voters. By 1988 the pendulum had swung so far in the other direction that Hollywood producers dictated the color scheme of the Democratic convention: mauve, beige, and Wedgwood blue instead of good old red, white, and blue. It made a great joke for Republicans.

While early television didn't have the technology for live coverage of events, it did have room for plenty of public-affairs programs such as "Meet the Press." (These were banished to Sunday mornings as sports began to fill weekend afternoons and entertainment took over prime time.) And the 1950s were a golden age for documentaries and exposés, two of the things that television does best.

Part documentary and part exposé, "See It Now" ran from 1951 to 1958 and had the same power that "60 Minutes" later enjoyed. Its creator and host was Edward R. Murrow, who had won fame during World War II as a CBS radio correspondent. ("See It Now" had its roots in Murrow's radio series, "Hear It Now.") Murrow distrusted television, but he knew how to use it as a weapon against injustice. Shortly after "See It Now" profiled a loyal military officer who was being discharged because of his *father's* political beliefs, the Air Force reinstated the young man. It was a triumph for Murrow and bitter gall for critics who thought that reporters had no right to question the U.S. government.

Most memorably, in 1954 "See It Now" tackled Senator Joseph McCarthy, who had ruined the careers of many Americans by falsely accusing them of being Communists. CBS management was nervous about airing the exposé and wouldn't promote it, so Murrow and his producer, Fred Friendly, paid for an ad in the *New York Times* themselves. Their program let McCarthy reveal himself in his own words. This tactic helped to turn the tide of opinion against the senator, who was soon on trial himself in army hearings. Television covered his downfall.

Murrow's critics wished he would stick to the celebrity interviews that made his other program, "Person to Person," so popular. Market forces and network timidity finally drove Murrow from television. "See It Now" and other regularly scheduled documentary series faded out as quiz shows became the rage.

By 1952 the use of television could make or break a politician. Presidential hopeful Adlai Stevenson, an eloquent man who balked at being "merchandised," bought thirty minutes of airtime for a speech. Unfortunately, he chose to preempt "I Love Lucy," which didn't endear him to viewers. His rival, General Dwight D. Eisenhower, reluctantly agreed to film

Edward R. Morrow, "the conscience of CBS"
© New York Daily News, used with permission

some twenty-second commercials. They were deceptively simple, yet clever:

> *Announcer:* Eisenhower answers America!
> *Citizen:* What about the cost of living, General?
> *Eisenhower:* My wife, Mamie, worries about the same thing. I tell her it's our job to change that on November fourth!

The same year, Richard Nixon brilliantly used television to save his career. While running for vice president, Nixon had been accused of skimming campaign funds for personal use. To clear his name, he made an emotional appeal on screen. Nixon ignored the main matter and spoke instead of his wife's frugality ("Pat doesn't have a mink coat."). He did admit taking one campaign gift, a family dog named Checkers. The "Checkers speech" went down in history as a triumph of image over issues.

Television news came of age in the early 1960s. Satellites made it possible to transmit instantly from anywhere in the world. Portable equipment made stories easier to report. Even the graphics were more sophisticated; news wasn't complete without "over the shoulder" pictures pioneered by ABC art director Ben Blank. The nightly news programs expanded from fifteen minutes to half an hour in 1962, just in time to cover a torrent of events.

The first presidential debate in 1960 was a landmark. A majority of radio listeners who were polled said Richard Nixon won. But television told a different story. John F. Kennedy looked confident and alert, while a sallow Nixon twitched and sweated. (The tanned Kennedy wore no makeup, while the small amount worn by Nixon wilted as he perspired.) Public opinion changed overnight, and the underdog Kennedy shot ahead—although Nixon technically "won" the next two debates.

"That night I learned TV was a very dangerous medium," said Don Hewitt, a "See It Now" alumnus who directed the debates. "We elected a president that night and we didn't have to wait to vote."

The assassination of President Kennedy on November 22, 1963, stunned the world. For four days, people gathered around their television sets to mourn and watch the events unfold. (All regular programs and commercials were suspended.) They saw Jacqueline Kennedy, the beautiful young widow, and they saw the assassin himself being murdered. At the funeral many wept at Kennedy's riderless horse and his young son's brave salute. Television and its anchors, especially CBS's Walter Cronkite, helped to hold America together when it might have exploded in grief.

Americans seemed to trust television more after Kennedy's assassination. Once newspapers and radio had been their chief source of news; now television was. Their first instinct in times of public crisis—assassinations, earthquakes, and (later) explosions in space—was to turn on the nearest set.

Kennedy's successor, Lyndon B. Johnson, inherited a nation about to explode in turmoil. Television news captured it all and often aroused action. Many viewers were inspired to support the Reverend Martin Luther King, Jr., who preached nonviolence, when they saw reports of police who brutally

The funeral of President John F. Kennedy on November 26, 1963.
His widow and children are at right. Kennedy's assassination
marked a turning point in American culture—since 1963, most
Americans have gotten their news from television rather than from
newspapers or radio.   © New York Daily News, used with permission

beat civil-rights workers. And images of the Vietnam War not only stirred the nation but helped to divide it.

American troops went to Vietnam to stop the spread of Communism in Southeast Asia. Seen on television, Vietnam did not look like a "good" war. It was the first widely televised war, and after 1965—when network news stopped broadcasting in black-and-white—its bloodshed and atrocities were seen "in living color." Many sights were gory: a Buddhist priest setting himself on fire in protest, a marine casually flicking his lighter to ignite a Vietnamese home into flames, and the impromptu street execution of a suspected Vietcong sympathizer by the chief of the South Vietnamese police in 1968.

Some viewers felt such coverage undermined America's war efforts. Others believed that television was merely reporting truths hidden by the government. Many wondered: what is this war turning us into?

In 1968 CBS made a radical move. It allowed Walter Cronkite to step out of his role as impartial news anchor, visit Vietnam, and come back with opinions on what he found. Cronkite, who ended each evening's news with an authoritative "And that's the way it is," surprisingly condemned the war. He said that America should withdraw because it could not win. Lyndon Johnson was listening and supposedly responded: "If I've lost Cronkite, I've lost middle America." He decreased the bombing of North Vietnam and declined to run for another term as president.

But peace did not yet return to Vietnam—or America. The slaying of Martin Luther King, Jr., in April 1968 sparked race riots in many cities. Two months later, in a terrible echo of his brother John's assassination, presidential hopeful Robert F. Kennedy was murdered. Enraged students shut down college campuses in protest against the war. Television news reported the steady stream of violence. Some called television an instigator.

The 1968 Democratic convention in Chicago became a showdown between old and young, liberal and conservative, government and media. The antiwar protesters and rabble-rousers were media smart: In front of television cameras they chanted, "The whole world is watching," to taunt the Chicago police and the National Guard. Fights also flared on the convention floor. When reporter Dan Rather was roughed up for no apparent reason, Walter Cronkite could not contain his disgust: "I think we've got a bunch of thugs here, Dan."

In fact, the whole world *was* watching, on television. What they saw was an America that seemed out of control.

Amid the mayhem of 1968, the conservative Richard Nixon emerged as president. Television had saved his career in 1952 and shattered it in 1960; now Nixon fought back. His vice president, Spiro T. Agnew, took every opportunity to lash out against the media. To Agnew, the people who decide what we see on the news—news directors, producers, and anchors—were "a tiny, enclosed fraternity of privileged men elected by no one." (He ignored the fact that if news staffs *were* elected, then broadcasting would become an arm of the government. That is forbidden by the First Amendment, which insures freedom of the press.)

The networks didn't like the attacks, yet they did some

soul-searching. They agreed that spy dramas and the few remaining Westerns might add to the climate of public violence, so many were canceled or toned down. Even the long-running "Gunsmoke" changed its opening shoot-out to a more peaceful confrontation.

Public disorder also helped to revive the documentary in a new form. In 1968 CBS introduced "60 Minutes," which combined tough investigative reporting and celebrity interviews. "A crook doesn't feel he's made it as a crook until he makes it onto "60 Minutes," Morley Safer has quipped. "If we can't get behind the [subject's] mask, it's not worth it," said executive producer Don Hewitt. The approach works: "60 Minutes" became the highest-rated and most profitable news show in history.

One event of the 1960s loomed above the rest. On July 20, 1969, a quarter of the world watched on television as Neil Armstrong became the first person to set foot on the moon. The landing was staged with the media in mind. Because the moon has no wind, the American flag planted there had been prerippled and made rigid for a good picture.

Network news had always been more of a public service than a bottom-line business. That began to change drastically in the 1970s, when giant corporations began buying networks and their affiliates. Suddenly news divisions had to pay their own way. Budgets were slashed, and news directors had to assign stories with ratings in mind.

The first response was to make newscasts look more like entertainment. Anchors, sportscasters, and weathermen be-

Live from 250,000 miles out in space: the 1969 moonwalk of U.S. astronauts Neil Armstrong and Edwin Aldrin. Because the moon has no wind, the flag was prestiffened to look good in pictures.
AP/Wide World Photos

gan bantering with each other on-screen, just like the "Today" gang. The emphasis shifted to "softer" news: regional happenings, consumer alerts, and health issues.

Independent stations also got into the act. They found it cheaper to produce their own news programs than to air movies or syndicated sitcom reruns. They could also offer something the networks couldn't: hometown features and community issues. In New Jersey, for example, reporters for WWOR-TV of Secaucus investigated a pattern of bias against black drivers on the northern end of the state turnpike, who were being stopped without clear cause far more often than whites.

While news formats were livelier, those who wanted to follow bigger stories in depth still had to wait for the network news at 7:00 or 7:30 P.M. There, not all the messages were upbeat. Vietnam still simmered, and one image seemed to be the last straw even for war supporters: footage of burned and naked Asian children running in terror from U.S. bomb attacks.

The networks, including PBS, were also the arena in which the world viewed the downfall of President Nixon. He and his staff tried to hide their involvement with the break-in at a Democratic party field–office at the Watergate Hotel in Washington, D.C., but their web of lies and corruption began to unravel at the Senate hearings, which were televised. The daily hearings were technical but fascinating; they drew more viewers than the soap operas. Perhaps remembering the success of his Checkers speech, Nixon made several televised appeals to the public. "I am not a crook," he insisted in one famous speech. By August 1975, when it was clear that he would be impeached, Nixon resigned. Gerald Ford took over. Jimmy Carter, former governor of Georgia, was elected U.S. president in 1976. At first he was dubbed "Jimmy Who?" because he was unknown beyond the South. But once Carter had won a few early primaries, he was labeled as a front-runner. The national exposure he got on television helped him win the election.

President Carter was undone by the Iranian hostage crisis, in which terrorists held fifty-three Americans captive in Teheran for 444 days. The captors understood the power of television: they bargained with the networks for film clips of the hostages and complained if Iran got too little coverage. The crisis made America feel humiliated, as well as hungry for information. In response, ABC launched a nightly update called "America Held Hostage," anchored by Ted Koppel. The program continued as "Nightline" after the hostages were released on the day of Ronald Reagan's inauguration. Its half-hour of late-night analysis became another landmark in television news.

Former actor Ronald Reagan has been called the Great Communicator and the first made-for-TV president. His campaign stops in 1980 and 1984 looked spontaneous, but every detail was carefully staged—from backdrops to balloons to cheering crowds. Questions from the press were not part of the plan. Reagan perfected the art of the sound bite with quips like this: "If my opponent's campaign were a TV show, it would be 'Let's Make a Deal.' You get to trade your prosperity for the surprise behind the curtain." (Reagan always said "my opponent" instead of publicizing the Democratic candidate's name.) He remained popular through the Iran-contra scandals that plagued his later years in office.

Always cutthroat, political campaigns became vicious in the 1980s. America is the only major Western country in which politicians must *buy* airtime to compete, and candidates paid millions to run ads. Many found that negative campaigning against an opponent worked better than positive messages. "The political process has been subverted by television," observed Don Hewitt, the CBS news veteran. "I'd outlaw political commercials if I could. I don't know if I'm voting for a candidate or a copywriter."

Network news also became a battleground. As one of six Republicans seeking the nomination for president, George Bush used a live interview with Dan Rather in 1988 to score points. Bush's media adviser sat off-camera and scrawled instant answers on cue cards to Rather's questions. Bush laced into Rather, looked tough, and surged in popularity. (Ironically, his main campaign promise was for a "kinder, gentler" America.)

Yet verbal battles may have been less serious than the rise in physical attacks against journalists. "We are the enemy—for both sides," said a camera operator who was assaulted in 1989 and 1990 while covering racial conflicts in Brooklyn, New York, and Teaneck, New Jersey.

Between 1980 and 1990, the once-mighty nightly news programs on ABC, CBS, and NBC lost half their viewers. There was plenty of competition. Local news covered the big stories earlier. "The MacNeil/Lehrer NewsHour" on PBS delivered a full hour of news and analysis. Even MTV had hourly newsbreaks. Some viewers were simply bored or burned out by so much news. Mainly, however, the "big three" bowed to the twenty-four-hour Cable News Network.

Founded as part of Ted Turner's cable empire in 1980, CNN has outlasted the early skeptics who called it "Chicken Noodle News." CNN earned its stripes when other news organizations seemed asleep at the switch. For example, because the networks had stopped covering space liftoffs, CNN was the only one to air the 1986 *Challenger* launch live and thus offer immediate coverage of its explosion. CNN also had a crew at the New Hampshire school of Christa McAuliffe, the teacher/astronaut killed in the tragedy. In 1989 alone CNN scooped the networks on some of the biggest events of the century: the San Francisco earthquake, the revolt of Chinese students in Tiananmen Square, and the fall of the Berlin Wall. Yet not even CNN has enough time or money to cover every event.

CNN made a misstep in 1990, when it asked viewers to vote by telephone for which stories should be featured. Groups with axes to grind clogged the lines, and some stories didn't get covered at all. News directors went back to doing the job. In *TV Guide*, Ted Koppel of "Nightline" explained the flaw in such ideas: "Almost no one [approaches] a television news program without an agenda. One of the responsibilities of the journalist on television is to try to identify what that agenda is and make sure the public knows about it."

CNN came of age during the Persian Gulf war in 1991.

Cable News Network came of age during the Persian Gulf war.
AP/Wide World Photos

CNN got the news faster than other networks did and quickly became the preferred, twenty-four-hour source of information around the world. And when Iraqi president Saddam Hussein forced reporters to leave his country, only CNN's Peter Arnett was allowed to stay. A controversy arose: had Arnett pulled off this coup by promising favorable coverage to the Iraqis? Arnett and CNN executives firmly denied that any such deal took place.

Actually, all news of the war in the Persian Gulf was heavily censored. Iraqi censors had to approve all television, newspaper, and radio coverage from Iraq. The United States issued press restrictions, too. Reporters on assignment had to be accompanied by U.S. Army escorts, and many allied operations were simply off-bounds to the press. U.S. officials believed that these rules would keep secret information from being leaked to enemies of Operation Desert Storm. They also feared the "Vietnam effect": that televising the pain and suffering of enemies might dilute American support for the war. For the same reasons, the United States had curbed press coverage when the United States invaded Grenada in 1983 and Panama in 1989.

While CNN chipped away at network supremacy so did local news programs. By the late 1980s independent stations could easily air high-quality national news by subscribing to video wire services and by employing uplinks to satellites for reports from great distances. Another source of "news" for many locals—the video news release, or VNR—was more controversial. VNRs look like impartial reports, but they can be biased toward the corporations that provide them free of charge. For example, after the tanker *Exxon Valdez* caused the worst oil spill in history, Exxon gave away VNRs that focused only on their cleanup efforts. The offer tempted many news directors who could not afford to send reporters to Alaska to cover the spill. They could make the VNR *look* like the station's own work by having one of their own reporters read the voice-over script, but the images came from Exxon.

Another dubious practice was dramatization. Using actors, costumes, and scenery, news directors sometimes simulated events for which there was no footage. The idea was to make the news easier to understand and to boost ratings. The practice ended on most news programs when viewers found it dishonest or confusing. But it continues on "reality-based" programs such as "A Current Affair," "Inside Edition," and "Hard Copy," which put a shock-value spin on the news. It is also a staple of sensationalized documentaries ("schlockumentaries") such as "Bad Girls," a hyped-up account of teenagers who pick fights.

Dramatizations work better on "America's Most Wanted," "Unsolved Mysteries," and other programs that investigate real cases. Viewers who believe they have information on these cases can call a special hotline number. One such tip led to the capture of John List, who had murdered his family eighteen years earlier. A few mistaken arrests have been made as a result of these investigations, but they have also solved hundreds of lesser crimes and missing-person cases. As one FBI agent has said: "Where else [but on television] can you interview forty million people at once?"

"America's Most Wanted" cast its electronic dragnet eighteen years into the past to help capture murderer John List. Pictured here are program host John Walsh (left) with Frank Bender, who made the sculpture that helped a viewer lead the FBI to the fugitive.
Courtesy STF Productions, Inc. Photo by Brian Davis

Reporters swarmed around William Kennedy Smith, who was
cleared of rape-and-battery charges in a televised trial that was one
of 1991's most-watched events. AP/Wide World Photos

VICTORY AND DEFEAT: 6

Sports and the Olympics

Sports and games have existed since ancient times. Television is new by comparison. Yet almost immediately they became so intertwined that it is hard to imagine one without the other.

Early television took viewers *to* the event. Cameras covered the action from the sidelines, and that was thrill enough, for a while. Despite the lack of fancy camerawork, viewers at the 1939 World's Fair were awestruck by the first major league baseball telecast, a doubleheader between the home team Brooklyn Dodgers and the Cincinnati Reds. The setup was so primitive that Dodgers announcer Red

Barber broadcast the games without a monitor to tell him where the two cameras were focused. Barber also ad-libbed three commercials, interviewed the players and managers on-camera between the games, and improvised a postgame wrapup, setting the pattern for virtually all live sports programs to come.

Better technology swept viewers *into* sports. It brought them "up close and personal," to use a phrase coined by "ABC Wide World of Sports." Even fans who attend events in person are often riveted to giant on-site screens or small personal sets. They may have come to the stadium for the big picture, but for close-ups nothing can beat video. Only the players have a closer view.

One of the main effects of television has been to create huge audiences for sports in general. In the early 1950s people bought sets just to watch baseball or roller derby (races on roller skates that were full of staged violence). Boxing and wrestling drew audiences every night of the week. Football took longer to catch on. To NBC and CBS, it wasn't a sport worth covering. Until the late 1950s they left it to low-rated ABC and the ailing Du Mont network, which asked teams to use a white ball for night games so viewers could follow the action in black-and-white.

The appetite for televised sports quickly proved bottomless. Broadcasting lesser-known sports was the response. Many Americans regarded hockey and soccer as foreign sports until television covered them. Golf and tennis were country-club games; skiing and yacht races were amusements for the rich. Competitive swimming and gymnastics were mainly school events. Auto racing (except for the Indianapolis 500)

Walter Lanier "Red" Barber, the dean of sportscasters, interviewed rookie infielder Jerry Lumpe in the New York Yankees' dugout in 1957.

was not popular outside the South, and bicycle racing was a European oddity. Today there are avid audiences around the world for all these sports and more—from car-wreck championships to bowling.

Many of these sports were added to viewers' menus by "ABC Wide World of Sports." Seen weekly since 1961, this two-hour video magazine presents "the thrill of victory, the agony of defeat" in all sports. ABC created it out of hunger, in the days when it owned only the rights to college football. Scouring the world for sports to cover, it presented a motley mix. There have been great moments: a perfect ice dance, a breathtaking ski jump. There have also been dumb stunts such as amateur "target diving" into a swimming pool, where paunchy men took turns jumping into a circle of balloons held in place by swimmers treading water.

Sublime or silly, "ABC Wide World of Sports" treats sports as entertainment. It was the first sports program to profile athletes closely—the personal side of "up close and personal." It also made an art of camera wizardry such as instant replay, freeze frames, and slow motion. Miniature cameras and microphones made it possible to broadcast from yachts and race cars and Alpine slopes, or to see a race as the runner runs it—and "ABC Wide World of Sports" was often the first program to use such equipment.

Buoyed by the success of its weekend sports coverage, ABC introduced "Monday Night Football" in 1970. Critics were skeptical that football could do well in prime time. But ABC focused on entertainment as well as sport, and early hosts Howard Cosell and Don Meredith soon became household names. Ratings eventually slipped, but "Monday Night

Football" endured, as much a part of American life as "I Love Lucy" or "Sesame Street."

When sports becomes entertainment, do players become entertainers? Television has brought fame to many athletes and ex-athletes, from Muhammad Ali to Joe DiMaggio to Peggy Fleming. It has also cast them in sports "specials" that border on farce, with hockey hulks trying their hand at tennis or quarterbacks attempting bicycle races.

Mainly, however, television has brought wealth to players. Their multimillion-dollar salaries elicit accusations of greed from some team owners, who must pay them. Players call it fair pay. Critics ask if television money has eroded sportsmanship. Harry Edwards, a sports sociologist at the University of California at Berkeley, told *Time* magazine that, because of television, "the eyes of the athlete have shifted from what you can do to challenge yourself, to how much money you can make."

Money aside, making sports "entertaining" sometimes results in overkill. Games and players can be lost in the swirl of interviews, color commentary, background bits, and computer graphics. Says Bill Morris, an Emmy Award–winning producer of sports videos and Olympic Games: "A thousand and one sidebars only divert attention from the main event." Harry Coyle, who produced baseball for decades at NBC, warns about the pitfalls of too much technology: "The only way a new innovation should be applied to live sports is if it's a plus factor for the coverage. . . . You're out there to bring all the action . . . in correct continuity to the public. When you do a ballgame, you're not doing *Star Wars*."

For sheer spectacle, of course, few productions can rival the Olympic Games. And they *are* spectacles, with the networks hiring pros such as David Wolper (better known as producer of the miniseries "Roots") to produce segments such as the opening ceremony.

Are the Olympics overproduced? Possibly. But the Games manage to transcend all the glittery parades and flag-raising ceremonies. National pride comes into play, as does a new level of competition. For a few weeks, the whole world seems to speak the same language. Even those indifferent to sports can find themselves hooked.

Thanks to television, many Olympic moments are sharply etched in popular history. In Lake Placid and at home, fans wept openly when Randy Gardner fell while skating in competition with partner Tai Babilonia during the 1980 Winter Games. Yet the spirits of an entire nation were revived during those Games when the underdog U.S. hockey team narrowly beat the Soviets and won the Gold Medal by beating Finland. The 1984 Summer Games in Los Angeles brought gasps of amazement when Zola Budd tripped Mary Decker during the women's 1,500-meter race—and gasps of admiration when Greg Louganis performed a perfect three-and-a-half back-somersault dive.

Broadcasting the Olympics is a colossal job. To cover the 1988 Winter Games, NBC sent six hundred people to Seoul, South Korea, for two weeks of broadcasts. The total cost was $100 million to produce the Games, plus $300 million for the rights. NBC paid $401 million just for the rights to the 1992 Summer Games in Barcelona, Spain. The price shocked the industry, but the network recouped some money by selling six hundred hours of coverage to three pay-per-view channels—

The Olympic Games are the premier showcase for world-class athletes such as Japanese skater Midori Ito. AP/Wide World Photos

although the main events would still be shown free on the NBC network. The Summer Games are worth more to networks, because they are longer and get higher ratings. They are also the ideal place to advertise the new fall programs.

Summer or winter, the world does watch the Olympics, and the stakes are high. This is partly why the Games abandoned their tradition of being for amateurs only, and why some athletes have risked their careers by drugging themselves in hopes of a better performance. It is also why the Olympics are used as a political arena. The 1972 Summer Games in Munich were overshadowed by Arab terrorists who murdered eleven Israeli athletes (five of the terrorists and a police officer were also killed). And American athletes were devastated when President Jimmy Carter reluctantly pulled the United States out of the 1980 Summer Games in Moscow. Carter felt he had no choice because the Soviet Union had invaded Afghanistan and was an ally of Iran, which was holding American hostages. NBC, which had paid $87 million for the broadcast rights, honored the boycott and did not televise the Games. Insurance covered 90 percent of the network's investment, but NBC still lost $20 million in travel and production costs.

Cable television introduced the first all-sports services, ESPN and SportsChannel, as well as several regional sports networks. In response, the broadcast networks (except Fox) and local stations have poured money into sports programming.

Whether over the air or on cable, television pays huge sums for the rights to broadcast sports. Broadcasters expect huge payoffs, both in viewership and ad revenue. In effect, television finances major league sports, so industry executives get to call many of the shots.

Perhaps more than any other sport, football has been shaped by television. And it's not just that kickoffs almost always take place after commercials, or that the National Football League recently put two more advertising time-outs into each game. A bigger example is that in 1990 the NFL agreed to add extra playoff games and extend its season by two weeks. That could push the Super Bowl into February, which happens to be one of the "sweeps" months, when the networks go all out for high ratings in order to raise their advertising rates. And when broadcasters looked for a way to extend football into the spring, the new World League of American Football was created.

In baseball, weekday games in many cities have become a thing of the past, because they can't be profitably televised. As in football, extra playoff games have lengthened the season. The World Series has been pushed from late September to early October to mid-October, when it can be too cold for comfortable play. If one contender is a West Coast team, games at that stadium will take place during twilight hours—prime time in New York—when it is difficult for the players to see.

Television breathed new life into hockey. In the late 1950s, only six pro hockey teams played in the United States. Now there are twenty-one. The National Hockey League changed the game's rules to expand pauses to thirty seconds, so that broadcasters could insert ads.

And in NBA pro basketball, the playoffs now include more

than half of all teams and can last for weeks. "Championships have lost some of their thrill and their meaning because television has spawned too many of them," says Red Barber.

Television has also changed the face of college sports. At schools with top teams, schedules are dictated by broadcasting needs. Putting the spotlight on football and basketball may mean that other sports—and especially women's sports—are ignored. Coaches and recruiters are under pressure to find the best players; their scholastic records don't always matter. Young athletes are lured by money and dreams of a pro career, but if they aren't pro material they may have nowhere to go after their college playing days are over.

The Super Bowl may be the biggest event created by and for television. After all, football had been around for almost one hundred years before this spectacle began in 1966. Super Bowl Sunday quickly grew into almost a national holiday, and the pregame show now lasts most of the day. It is television's most expensive ad buy: in 1991 thirty seconds of airtime cost $800,000, and advertisers may spend half a million dollars more to produce special commercials just for the game. Yet even the Super Bowl is not immune to ups and downs. Viewership reached 118 million in 1991, up from 74 million the year before. However, the 1990 match-up of the San Francisco 49ers versus the Denver Broncos was considered somewhat lopsided.

While the Super Bowl may embody sports at its most commercial, it is also free—so far—for anyone with a television

Members of the victorious New York Giants and the defeated Buffalo Bills prayed together in a circle after Super Bowl XXV. The 20–19 contest was a programmer's dream.   AP/Wide World Photos

set. This is no longer true of all major sports events. Premium cable and pay-per-view have become the norm for top boxing bouts, and viewers who want to catch all of any team's games almost always need basic and premium service.

Will sports slowly disappear from noncable channels? Some Americans fear this, and they have pushed for laws to fight it. Charles Schumer, U.S. Representative (Dem., N.Y.), introduced the Baseball Viewers Protection Act of 1989, whereby major league teams with cable contracts would have to broadcast at least half their games on free stations. The U.S. Congress also held hearings that year to determine if consumers were hurt by the shift of many sports to cable.

Both moves made news, but not policy. The lawmakers may have wanted to prod the cable industry into policing itself. Government will need to remain a watchdog if the outlook of some cable executives is any sign. John Mohr, president of SportsChannel Regional Networks, told *Channels* magazine: "It doesn't say anything in the Bill of Rights about a citizen's right to watch his favorite team."

On free and pay television, one trend is likely to last: sponsors will keep attaching their names to sports events, such as the Federal Express Orange Bowl and the Mobil Cotton Bowl. This practice is good for corporate image, the sponsors say, and it boosts employee morale. And for tobacco companies, sports sponsorship is one of the few ways to get airtime. Ads for cigarettes and cigars have been banned on television since 1971, but logos are not banned. This can be a gold mine: during the 1989 Marlboro Grand Prix, Marlboro's logo could be seen on the screen 49 percent of the time.

vvvvvvvvvvvvvvvvvvvvv

Television and sports have changed radically since NBC came to the Brooklyn Dodgers in 1939 and pleaded for permission to televise a game. Money never entered into that agreement. Fifty years later, facing stiff competition for ratings from cable television, CBS paid the equivalent of a million dollars per inning for the four-year broadcast rights to the major league baseball playoffs, the World Series, and a prime-time "Game of the Week." Other networks complained that CBS paid far too much, but the deal set off broadcast bidding wars in every major league sport, college sports, and the Olympics. When CBS took a huge loss on its investment, the spending sprees died down, and sports lost some of their luster as entertainment—at least in prime time.

SMALL THINGS CONSIDERED:

7

Children's Television

In the first days of television, many children's programs came on early in the evening. Programmers envisioned that Mom, Dad, and all the kids would cozily gather around the set after dinner. Little did they suspect that television would later be accused of driving families apart.

The first shows for children, like those for adults, had the freshness that came with live television. They weren't slick, but they were lively. And while kids were regarded as consumers even then, the huge advertising and merchandising industry that grew around children's television was still small.

"If television were working, kids would want to go out and clean up the rivers, help the hungry and the homeless, and would know that peace is a good thing and nuclear war is the end of the world."
—Peggy Charren, founder and president, Action for Children's Television

"We try to get the kids to watch educational TV, but it's always on opposite entertainment."
—Marge Simpson of "The Simpsons," "interviewed" in *TV Guide*

Becky (Danielle Marcot) is mesmerized by the magical 18-inch high Mr. Conductor (George Carlin) on the award—winning PBS series "Shining Time Station."

© 1991 Quality Family Entertainment, Inc. Photo by Lia Falzon

Howdy Doody was television's first superstar, preceding even Milton Berle. The freckled marionette was part of a circus troupe headed by human host Buffalo Bob Smith. (Chief Thunderthud's characteristic cry was one that would be adopted some forty years later by the Teenage Mutant Ninja Turtles: "Cowabunga!") Seen daily for almost nine years, "Howdy Doody" set the pattern for many national and local shows to follow: puppets, skits, songs, cartoons, short films, a genial master of ceremonies, and an on-stage audience of kids to shriek and clap and join in the fun.

As viewers outgrew the antics of Doodyville, they turned in the mid-1950s to "The Mickey Mouse Club," one of ABC's first hits. Produced by Walt Disney Studios, this show had a secret weapon in its cartoon characters: Mickey Mouse and Donald Duck were movie favorites but had never been seen on television. Disney Studios expanded its success with "Disneyland," which lasted on network television (under various titles) from 1954 until the creation of the Disney Channel for cable in 1983. "Davy Crockett," a segment within "Disneyland," also gave rise to one of television's first merchandising crazes: by early 1955, every boy in America wanted a coonskin cap like Davy's.

"Kukla, Fran and Ollie," created by puppeteer Burr Tillstrom, was another early favorite. Kukla (Russian for "doll") and Ollie (Oliver J. Dragon) were among ten Kuklapolitan Players who visited each evening with actress Fran Allison. Sometimes Fran and the puppets staged their own show-within-a-show, such as "Martin Dragon, Private Tooth," but mostly they chatted in a low-key way. Jim Henson has said that the Kuklapolitan Players helped inspire the

Muppets—high praise for low-tech puppets who rarely followed a script.

Two misters made their mark in early television. "Mr. I Magination," played by author Paul Tripp, was a train engineer who acted out fantasies sent in by viewers. And for fourteen years, Don Herbert coaxed families to "Watch Mr. Wizard" as he used common household items in science experiments.

Children's drama got off to a memorable start with "Captain Video and His Video Rangers," a daily science-fiction series. It had all the special effects that could be concocted on a prop budget of twenty-five dollars per week. But viewers loved it anyway, and they eagerly mailed away for decoder rings and space helmets. "The Adventures of Superman" showcased another superhero, one who had been around since 1938 in comic strips, radio, and the movies. Superman and his alter ego, mild-mannered reporter Clark Kent, were played by George Reeves. The program's comic-book exaggeration offered a change from the noble animal dramas aimed at young viewers: "Fury," "My Friend Flicka," "Rin Tin Tin," and, of course, "Lassie," about a loyal collie with a heart of gold.

Almost as soon as children's television began, so did complaints about it. A particular worry was that preschoolers weren't being served. NBC reacted with "Ding Dong School," a daily learning program hosted by respected educator Dr. Frances Horwich, and CBS offered Robert Keeshan's "Captain Kangaroo," which followed the standard formula of skits, cartoons, and puppets. The Captain still had a strong viewership when CBS replaced him with an early-morning news program after thirty years.

One of the people who wanted to improve children's television was a young man named Fred Rogers. One of his early jobs was to help organize America's first community-based educational TV station, WQED in Pittsburgh, Pennsylvania. WQED wanted a children's program that would entertain as well as teach. When no one else came forward to create it, Rogers did. "Children's Corner," hosted by Josey Carey, evolved into "Mister Rogers' Neighborhood." It has not changed much—even Daniel Striped Tiger is the same puppet sewn for the original show in 1954—except that Mr. Rogers himself became the host. Quiet and patient, he has always been a respite of calm in a frenzied world. Comedians have mimicked his soft-spoken style, but even those who mock him seem to love him. No emotion or fear is silly in Mr. Rogers's eyes.

"Sesame Street" changed children's television. Created by Joan Ganz Cooney and Children's Television Workshop in 1969, it had a goal different from any other program's: to educate disadvantaged preschoolers. It is set in a city neighborhood, not in suburbia or a fantasyland. It made Jim Henson's Muppets as much a part of childhood as Mickey Mouse or Winnie the Pooh. The quick-cut use of skits, songs, and animation was radically new. So was a program "sponsored" by letters or numbers.

While widely praised, "Sesame Street" also drew criticism. Many educators found it *too* fast-paced and fragmented. Classroom teachers worried that they couldn't compete with Kermit and Big Bird. Some adults felt it focused on skills at the expense of feelings. In response, "Sesame Street" made some segments longer, strengthened plot lines, and gave viewers more time to respond to on-screen questions. And it spent more time on ideas such as love, birth, death, and cultural diversity.

Over the years, children's television has become an industry in which advertisers call the shots. And advertisers say that "quality" children's programs rarely draw enough viewers to be profitable. It's odd, then, that "Sesame Street"—a proven success seen by billions of viewers in eighty countries—hasn't been copied by the networks. It's also odd that this noncommercial program has been accused of being too commercial. Certainly it fuels a huge spinoff industry of books, toys, clothing, and other merchandise, but these licenses help pay for the program.

"Sesame Street" can silence the critics by pointing to its results. Study after study has shown that "Sesame Street" does give preschoolers a head start. It is a sound way to reach and teach children—and probably the cheapest way, as the late Jim Henson once said. And finally, it also boosted family entertainment by launching the Muppets.

After the success of "Sesame Street," Children's Television Workshop introduced "The Electric Company" for ages six to eleven. CTW also serves preteens and teenage viewers with "Square One Television" (dubbed "Math meets MTV") and "3-2-1 Contact," a daily magazine about science.

Cartoons are a staple of children's television. The best ones are silly and witty enough to entertain kids and adults alike.

Mathematical know-how helps solve mysteries on "Mathnet," a
"Dragnet" spoof on CTW's "Square One TV."   CTW/Richard Termine.
© Children's Television Workshop, 1991

"What we tried to do was amuse ourselves," said pioneer Mel Blanc, the original voice of Bugs Bunny, Woody Woodpecker, Daffy Duck, Porky Pig, Tweety, Sylvester, Barney Rubble, Dino the Dinosaur, and hundreds of other animated characters. "We didn't make pictures for children. We didn't make pictures for adults. We made them for ourselves."

The earliest television cartoons came straight from the movies. (In the 1930s and 1940s, cartoons always ran before feature films.) But soon animation studios were making cartoons just for television. Networks found it cheaper to buy and rerun cartoons than to produce live shows. New characters such as Jay Ward's Crusader Rabbit ("star" of the first made-for-TV cartoon) and Hanna-Barbera's Huckleberry Hound joined classics from Walt Disney, Warner Brothers, Walter Lantz Studios, and Terrytoons. "Rocky and His Friends," also created by Ward, entertained all ages with its pun-filled Fractured Fairy Tales, Aesop's Fables, and the adventures of Rocky and Bullwinkle. Animators even snuck in some history ("Hector Heathcote") and science ("Tennessee Tuxedo and His Friends").

With the exception of "Huckleberry Hound," which ran in the early evening (and even won an Emmy Award in 1959), television cartoons were confined to early mornings and late afternoons until the 1960s. Then programmers experimented in prime time with "The Flintstones," "The Jetsons," and "Top Cat." These cartoons succeeded as family viewing, along with several other prime-time programs that kids could enjoy, from "The Patty Duke Show" to "Bewitched." But early-evening family programs such as "Kukla, Fran and Ollie" were gone, replaced by news. The networks carried almost no evening programs primarily intended for young viewers. Those were relegated to Saturday mornings and weekday afternoons.

When critics argue about the lack of quality in children's television, they point to Saturday mornings. Many of the cartoons, they say, offer no food for thought; they are merely junk food for the mind. There are too many superheroes, too much violence, too many stereotypes, and too few female characters.

Some programs, like Mattel's "Hot Wheels," are little more than thirty-minute ads for cereals and toys. The FCC has refused to act decisively against product-based programs. For example, stations cannot include commercials for any G.I. Joe products during "G.I. Joe," but they can run such commercials immediately *after* the show.

However, Action for Children's Television (ACT) helped convince the U.S. government to limit advertising and to pressure broadcasters about quality in children's programs. In 1991 the FCC put stricter limits on the amount of advertising permitted in shows produced primarily for viewers under the age of twelve. The maximum is 10.5 minutes of commercials per hour on weekends and 12 minutes per hour on weekdays. Also, all stations (except PBS stations) must report on their efforts to provide "educational and informational" programming when applying for the renewal of their licenses. "This gives parents and others a hook by which they can hold television stations accountable for kids," said ACT founder Peggy Charren, who disbanded the group in 1992.

ACT and other advocates tried for years to raise the standard of children's programming. They succeeded briefly in the 1970s. Fran Allison and Burr Tillstrom's puppets returned to television at that time as hosts of "CBS Children's Film Festival," and Bill Cosby got into the cartoon act with "Fat Albert and the Cosby Kids," about a gang that helped other kids solve problems. Such programs won awards for quality, but few won high ratings and advertising support. Attempts to revive classics such as "Howdy Doody" and "Kukla, Fran and Ollie" in the 1960s and 1970s also failed. These programs now seemed too dated and too naive for television.

As the award-winners disappeared, superhero cartoons crept back into weekend schedules. And new protests arose over the amount of aggression in them. Threatened with government regulation, cartoon producers initiated their own changes. They toned down violence and removed guns, threats, and physical jeopardy. On the whole, cartoons are tamer than they once were—although some people feel they have become sanitized and unrealistic.

Yet another uproar arose in the 1980s over two "interactive" programs: Mattel's "Captain Power" and Axlon's "Moto Monsters and the Tech-Force." The programs emitted inaudible signals that allowed viewers to shoot at targets on the screen—not with guns, of course, but with "shooting toys" such as spaceships. Toy makers insisted that viewers didn't have to own the toy to enjoy the show. The argument didn't convince parents who were being badgered to buy the toys, however.

Along with superheroes, there has always been room for

softer cartoons that appeal to preschoolers, such as "The Smurfs" and "The Care Bears." Prime-time programs and movies often find new life in animated versions, from "Back to the Future" and "Beetlejuice" to Roseanne Arnold's "Little Rosey" (which was canceled when Arnold refused to add male characters so that the show would appeal to boys). Popular musical groups such as the Beatles and New Kids on the Block inspire cartoons, and so do games ("The Super Mario Bros. Super Show!") and books ("Where's Waldo?").

Kids deserve more than cartoons based on recycled ideas. Every generation needs its imagination teased by an oddball host, and from the late 1980s to the early 1990s there was only one: Paul Reubens, better known as Pee-wee Herman and the creator of "Pee-wee's Playhouse." There are few attempts to duplicate public television's "Wonderworks," a film anthology, or "Reading Rainbow," which gets kids hooked on books. Networks have begun to realize that Saturday mornings are glutted with cartoons. Even so, there have been few experiments with other kinds of formats in this time slot, even safe ones like music videos and sports. Programmers have even turned down surefire hits—such as the series based on Ann M. Martin's phenomenally popular fiction series "The Baby-sitters Club"—because they want shows that appeal primarily to boys. ("The Baby-sitters Club" was picked up by the pay-cable service HBO.)

If anything, the cartoon battle has shifted to weekday afternoons. The hours of 3:00 P.M. to 5:00 P.M. are kids' prime time. "Teenage Mutant Ninja Turtles," subject of a monster hit movie, started here. The huge success of Disney's "Duck Tales" and "Chip 'n' Dale's Rescue Rangers" led to "Tailspin" (from Rudyard Kipling's *Jungle Book*) and "Darkwing Duck." So many kids tuned in to the "Disney Afternoon" that Warner Brothers joined the competition with new "Merrie Melodies Classics" and "Tiny Toons Adventures" produced by Steven Spielberg. His television cartoons recall the best of the old days. They are full of rambunctious humor and slapstick action, without weapons. Not to be outdone, Fox launched its own Kids Network with "Peter Pan and the Pirates."

However, afternoons offer little quality drama aside from the occasional "ABC Afterschool Special," "CBS Schoolbreak Special," or "NBC Project Peacock." Most are about adolescent and family crisis issues: bulimia, drug abuse, gambling, sexual orientation, date rape, adult illiteracy, sexually transmitted diseases, or alcoholic parents. They are well-meaning but sometimes too obvious; the emphasis is on quick scenes and hopeful (if not happy) endings. For teen drama that avoids clichés, the field has been limited to "DeGrassi Junior High" and "Clarissa Explains It All," as well as prime-time offerings such as "Beverly Hills 90210."

The advent of cable television in the 1970s promised more and better shows for children. Was it just a sales pitch to families and governments?

Nickelodeon, the first children's channel, was ad-free when it began in 1979. Cable operators footed the bills. Nickelodeon introduced a grand array of programs that were entertaining and educational: "Reggie Jackson's World of

"Clarissa Explains It All" in one of television's more realistic young-adult dramas, starring Melissa Joan Hart.

Sports," "Pinwheel" (an "electronic sandbox" for preschoolers), "Livewire" (a talk show for teens), "You Can't Do That
on Television" (slapstick humor), "What Will They Think of
Next?" (science), and even claymation by Will Vinton, creator of the California Raisins. The channel also imported
some good dramas and brought Mr. Wizard (Don Herbert)
back to television after an absence of fourteen years.

Advertising came to Nickelodeon, and so did an ownership
change that meant fewer new programs and more reruns.
"Nick at Nite" revived "Mr. Ed," "The Donna Reed Show,"
"Green Acres," "My Three Sons," and other shows from the
1960s and 1970s. Yet the channel still aims high and sometimes reaches its mark. It created the imaginative "Eureeka's
Castle," one of the few preschool programs to rival those of
the Children's Television Workshop. It keeps ads to a mini-
mum—as little as eight minutes per hour. And it still stretches
its boundaries with new game shows, news programs, and
cartoons such as "Doug," which bypasses superheroes to ex-
plore the adventures of an ordinary eleven-year-old boy.

The Disney Channel, a premium pay service, has helped
fulfill the promise of cable. Of course, with sole rights to
Disney characters, it didn't have to start from scratch. But the
channel has never been content to rest on its reruns. It is a
showcase for new cartoons, family films, and programs such
as "You and Me, Kid," one of the few designed for adults and
children to watch and participate in together.

Home Box Office also features good children's programming, from "Babar" cartoons to Jim Henson's "The Ghost of
Faffner Hall." And there is a fair amount of children's and
family fare—some good, some not—on Showtime, the reli

Linda Ellerbee keeps kids informed with "Nickelodeon Special Editions." The cable network was the first to offer news and current events specials exclusively for young viewers.

gious Family Channel, the nature-loving Discovery Channel, and WTBS. And Ted Turner stepped up his commitment to kids with "Captain Planet and the Planeteers"—a cartoon with a strong pro-environmental message and tie-in toys in recyclable packages.

THE BUSINESS SIDE:

Advertisers, Programming, Ratings

ommercial television is a big business. As with any other business, its goal is to make money. It's said in jest that the industry motto is "Keep the ratings up, the costs down, and the government out." Program quality rarely enters into the equation.

Television is also a tough business. Literally millions of people keep an eye on it—the government, advertisers, and viewers. In America, networks and stations are licensed to operate "in the public interest, convenience and necessity," but mainly they answer to their shareholders.

Sometimes, on big issues, the

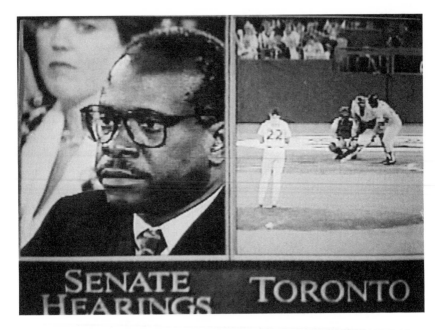

October 1991: While other networks preempted all programs to carry the Clarence Thomas Supreme Court confirmation hearings, CBS offered split-screen updates. CBS had invested millions for baseball rights and did not want to drop the American League play-offs. AP/Wide World Photos

U.S. Congress does step in. For instance, it banned cigarette advertising in 1971 and set guidelines to reduce commercials in children's programming in 1990. But for the most part, the industry runs itself.

Advertising money is the lifeblood of commercial television. Each year advertisers spend over $20 billion to buy airtime to run commercials. This is what makes over-the-air television "free," but it isn't really free. Viewers pay for television by buying what is advertised on it. Cable subscribers also pay monthly fees, which is one reason that cable networks are in a stronger financial position than NBC, CBS, and ABC.

In the 1950s, big-money advertisers ran the show. They named programs after themselves: "The Camel News Caravan," "The Kraft Music Hall," "Texaco Star Theater." They arranged prime-time schedules, and the networks meekly agreed. They also made routine demands that seem absurd today. For instance, because it was sponsored by a cigarette maker, "The Camel News Caravan" couldn't show NO SMOKING signs or people smoking cigars. (They did make an exception for Winston Churchill, the British leader never seen without his cigar.) Gas chambers couldn't be mentioned in a "Playhouse 90" drama about the Jewish Holocaust because the program was sponsored by gas companies.

Advertisers began to lose their clout when single-sponsor programs became too expensive. For decades it has been cheaper and more strategic to air one ad on eight different programs than eight different ads on one program. Also, the networks took firmer control after the quiz-show scandals of the 1950s. And advertisers have other problems to worry about, such as reaching the people who tape programs and zap past commercials altogether.

Advertisers have only one direct way to control programming. If they dislike a program or episode—usually because they feel it makes their product look bad—they can refuse to sponsor it. For instance, beer companies won't buy time on a program about drunk driving, and pizza chains don't like on-screen blood because they're afraid it reminds viewers of tomato sauce. But advertisers cannot change a program or stop it from airing, and usually the network can find another sponsor.

Yet, in a twist of logic, advertisers have become targets for groups who are unhappy with television. These people feel that the networks don't listen to them but that advertisers can't afford not to.

Pressure groups come in all shapes and sizes, from minorities and parent-teacher associations to labor unions and religious groups. Some feel they are unfairly portrayed on television. Others believe that television is unwholesome, violent, or otherwise on the wrong track. Some of the most vocal opponents have been fundamentalist Christians who target sponsors of programs they find unacceptable. (Even tame programs such as "The Magical World of Disney" and "The Wonder Years" have been criticized for such issues as disrespect to parents.) Protesters blanket sponsors with letters and may refuse to buy their products.

When threatened with boycotts, advertisers try to listen. In the 1970s Owen B. Butler, chairman of the board of Procter

& Gamble, America's biggest advertiser, scolded broadcasters for their use of "gratuitous sex, violence, and profanity." The networks then tried a special family hour of wholesome programs from 8:00 P.M. to 9:00 P.M. But most were flops in the ratings, and that didn't please advertisers either. Violence also increased on shows aired after 9:00 P.M. The family hour quietly faded.

The industry's self-policing efforts have also dwindled. Each network once had a powerful standards and practices department that acted as a censor. It weeded out or toned down political opinions, racism, sexism, violence, and vulgarity. It could reject programs or demand changes. The network was like a strict parent, and some writers and producers saw themselves as rebels. They would throw in a little profanity as a bargaining chip.

Those games are mostly over. Today only ABC has a standards and practices department; the other networks have merged theirs into programming or community relations. Standards have eased in response to social changes and the desire to compete with more adult fare on cable television.

What viewers see, and when they see it, is decided by programming executives at each network or station. It is far from a logical process.

Networks and cable stations don't create most of their own programs, except for the news. They buy them from outside producers with good track records. These producers try to pitch new ideas in terms of old favorites. Thus "True Colors" was described as "an interracial "Brady Bunch" and "Married . . . with Children" as "not the Cosbys."

Most new program ideas are rejected. A few others seem so surefire that networks buy them without a sample episode—called a pilot—or even a sample script. (This happened with "Green Acres" and "In the Heat of the Night," because the producers had hits running and the stars were well known.)

If an idea seems promising, the network usually orders a pilot episode and tests it for studio or cable audiences. Some test audiences are shown a cartoon first, just to make sure they have a good sense of humor! While watching the pilot, the viewers turn a dial from 0 to 100 to register their likes and dislikes. A score of 70 is considered good, and the programmers study the highs and lows very carefully. If the overall score is bad, the pilot may never make it to the air.

"Testing is a tool, not an end-all," said Fred Silverman, a former executive at NBC, CBS, and ABC and an independent producer. "For example, 'Hill Street Blues' tested terribly—the audience had trouble with the overlapping plot lines and was upset when the two most likeable characters died." But NBC executives loved the program, so those characters were written back into "Hill Street Blues" before it premiered. It eventually became a huge hit, as did other notable test failures such as "Family Ties," "Cheers," and "Miami Vice."

Low-testing programs may make it to the air because of contract obligations ("Cop Rock") or prestige ("Twin Peaks"). Hunches also play a part. The comedy "Sister Kate" tested poorly but NBC entertainment president Brandon Tartikoff went with it partly because his seven-year-old daughter liked it. (It flopped.) Fox tried to ride the coattails of "Twin Peaks" with a documentary, "American Chronicles," by the same producers. Fox Entertainment president Peter Chernin told *TV Guide* candidly: "I think the audience is looking for something like this but maybe not. I don't know." They weren't; the show never got out of the ratings cellar.

Because the tried-and-true is less risky than the innovative, television copies from itself without shame. It also borrows from movies, from *M*A*S*H* to *Parenthood*, which is not surprising since many film studios are also in the television production business. Yet as viewers spread themselves across dozens of channels, some programmers do gamble and win. By taking a chance on "Twin Peaks," ABC won publicity if not high ratings.

If network programming is predictable, cable is more so. Entire stations are based on the past. "Ha! Comedy TV" seemed like a fresh idea, but it was packed with old episodes of "The Three Stooges," "The Lucy Show," "Rhoda," and "Saturday Night Live." (The channel later became part of Comedy Central, which did offer more than reruns.) Nickelodeon's "Nick at Nite" has done a better job of packaging reruns into "TV Land." But cable has created relatively few new series of its own, and the prospects are bleak. Fred Silverman observed that "full-service cable entertainment channels look like network has-beens."

Another big part of programming is scheduling. The challenge is to fit the program to the time slot in which it will shine. One method is block programming, whereby networks try to lure and hold viewers with a string of similar shows. NBC successfully block-programmed Thursday nights

A parade of Donna Reed clones welcomed "The Donna Reed Show" to the Nick at Nite lineup. "Make your beds!" they called to amused onlookers during the publicity stunt, which took place in Chicago. "Clean your rooms!"   Photograph courtesy of Nickelodeon.

as its comedy night for years, with "The Cosby Show," "A Different World," and "Cheers" as the linchpins.

Another programming trick is to schedule a promising new show immediately after a proven hit; ABC tried this by following "Roseanne" with "Coach." A weak series may be "hammocked" between stronger ones, or it may be hop-scotched from night to night in search of an audience. That strategy can backfire, though, when shows switch time slots so often that viewers give up on finding them.

Programmers are always looking over their shoulders at the competition. If ABC, CBS, and Fox feature comedy at a certain hour, NBC may counter-program a hot new drama. Or it may dilute everyone's ratings by trying a comedy of its own. Guerrilla tactics are uncommon but fun. After "The Simpsons" caught on, Fox boldly pitted it against "The Cosby Show," which had topped the ratings for six years. "Cosby" fought to keep its lead, losing valuable ratings points to the animated upstart.

Television gets a report card every morning, in the form of the previous day's ratings. This fact helps explain why the industry is such a nervous one.

Ratings are all–important in commercial television because they determine how much money the networks and stations charge for advertising. The more viewers, the higher the price. That's why it costs almost a million dollars to buy thirty seconds of airtime on the Super Bowl but only a few thousand on "Meet the Press." (If a show doesn't actually gain the number of viewers expected, the advertiser gets a "make good," or a free time in the future for another commercial.)

Billions of dollars hinge on ratings, yet only a handful of homes are actually measured. Of about 90 million homes in the United States with televisions, the A. C. Nielsen Company surveys only about 5,700 of them—about 1 in every 16,000 households. These viewers are chosen at random and paid a small fee. (Ratings are also measured by Arbitron, Inc., but Nielsen's ratings are more widely used.)

Nielsen measures viewership in two ways. Each "ratings point" represents about 931,000 households. (The figure varies slightly from year to year.) The "share" is the percentage of actual sets tuned in. These figures can be used as a kind of scorecard.

Here's a sample:

Thursday, June 20, 1991, 8:00 P.M.–8:30 P.M.

Program	Network	Number of Viewers	Ratings Points	Share	Rank for Week
The Cosby Show	NBC	14.9 million	10.5	22	28
The Simpsons	Fox	14.1 million	8.6	18	47
Top Cops	CBS	10.3 million	7.4	15	58
Father Dowling Mysteries	ABC	9.8 million	7.3	15	60

Of all households with their sets on at that time, 22 percent (indicated by the 22 share), or 14.9 million viewers, were tuned into "The Cosby Show." The show ranked 28th among 92 programs for that week. (The most-watched program that week was "Cheers," with a 27 share, while two shows tied for last place: "Alien Nation" and "The Los Altos Story.") "The Cosby Show" beat "The Simpsons" that night, with "Top Cops" and "Father Dowling Mysteries" trailing behind. The 30 percent of viewers who weren't watching CBS, ABC, NBC, or Fox were spread among all the other channels.

Nielsen measures more widely during the "sweeps months" of November, February, May, and July. That's when local stations set their ad rates, so that's when programmers roll out their big guns. During the sweeps, every station is thick with lavish specials and miniseries, murder and mayhem, sex, violence, and fad diets. On soap operas, weddings take place and long-awaited babies are born. The news looks different, too: it's crammed with sensational reports like "Can You Trust Your Baby-Sitter?" and "Is Your Town's Water Killing You?"

The sweeps are also frenzied because that's when Nielsen more closely measures exactly who is watching and buying. What sex are they? What age? What is their highest level of education? Their household income? Are they urban, suburban, or rural? Advertisers have to target their audiences, and numbers alone are no longer enough.

In general, audiences are changing. People with more education used to watch less television, but that's no longer true. The average white family in the United States watches about fifty hours a week. Black households usually watch seventy-seven hours a week. Housebound people—children and the elderly—are among the most faithful viewers.

Yet viewers aged eighteen to thirty-four count most in the television business, because they spend more on consumer products. Fox's appeal to this age group helped account for its early success. If a show has middling ratings but strong

Rolland Smith, winner of seven Emmy Awards, left "The CBS Morning Program" to anchor the "10 O'Clock News" on WWOR-TV. Like many independent stations, New Jersey–based WWOR holds its own against the bigger networks. © New York Daily News, used with permission

eighteen-to-thirty-four demographics, it's less likely to be canceled.

While the Nielsen system has been the industry standard, the industry has questioned its accuracy. Readings are taken automatically at some sample homes, while at others, viewers must punch in personal code numbers or jot their program choices in special diaries. It's feared that many people simply don't bother to do these things.

Another shortcoming is that Nielsen has been slow to measure VCR playback use and to keep track of viewing in college dormitories, hotels, nursing homes, workplaces, or on battery-operated sets. Because every viewer translates into dollars, networks want these hidden audiences counted.

Even with its flaws, the ratings system has been slow to change. A new system would be expensive, and financially strapped networks are reluctant to foot the bill. Another point in the system's favor is that it is objective. When ABC threatened to drop Nielsen and do its own audience surveys, advertisers wouldn't go along.

From the audience's standpoint, the biggest problem with ratings may be that they don't measure how viewers feel about a show. "Just because you don't have a Nielsen box on your set does not mean you do not have a voice or a valid opinion," said Dorothy Swanson, president and founder of Viewers for Quality Television. VQT began as a grass-roots effort to return "Cagney & Lacey" to the air. Letter-writing campaigns by VQT members and other fans helped convince cable networks to "uncancel" "Beauty and the Beast," "Frank's Place," and other quality programs that the networks had killed. Swanson noted that classics like "60

Minutes," "All in the Family," and "M*A*S*H" were rated poorly at first; "Cheers" ended its first year tied for seventy-third place in a field of ninety-eight. "Good shows can take time to find an audience," Swanson said.

Prime-time television is expensive to produce. Half-hour sitcoms such as "A Different World" cost half a million dollars or more per show. Hour-long dramas cost $1 million or more; some episodes of "Moonlighting" cost almost $3 million.

About a third of these costs pay for the cast and for production facilities. Another 15 to 20 percent is split among producer, director, and writers. The rest goes to the production and camera staffs, electrical expenses, film laboratory and editing fees, set design and construction, wardrobe, makeup and hair stylists, music, and any special effects. Everything has a price tag. For example, producers of "The New Zorro" spent four thousand dollars each season on black dye to make sure that Zorro's horse looked jet-black on camera.

When networks buy a series, they pay for two showings of each episode. To earn back their investment, they sell airtime for commercials; usually they don't break even and earn a profit until the second showing. The big money is made by the producers, who lease—or syndicate—programs to nonnetwork stations and broadcasters in foreign countries for rerun. In the New York area WWOR paid $30 million to the producers of "The Cosby Show" for forty-two months of reruns, and other local stations paid big sums for them, too. Cosby himself, who owns a stake in the program, made an estimated $250 million from those sales.

Television earnings can be astronomical. Creators of a drama, comedy, or variety program—the people whose names appear before the show begins—are paid royalties every time the show is aired, anywhere in the world. Salaries are huge at the very top: Sam Donaldson, Connie Chung, Barbara Walters, Diane Sawyer, Jane Pauley, and network entertainment presidents all make more than $1 million per year. Tom Brokaw, Peter Jennings, and Bryant Gumbel are in the $2 million range; Dan Rather earned $3.4 million in 1991. But stratospheric sums are not common. The average TV news reporter on an independent station makes around $35,000. Sports commentators average about $40,000, weathercasters a bit more.

Those who are talented and lucky can get rich in television. But plenty of talented television people don't earn much more than people in other professions.

QUALITY AND QUANTITY:

Public Television and Cable Television

*P*ublic television in America is best known for three things: "Sesame Street," lots of culture and serious talk, and, usually, no commercials. Some viewers are so devoted to it that they rarely watch anything else. Others find it dull or snobbish.

Public television has always been accused of not offering much for the average viewer. Its audience does tend to be more educated, but as an editorial in the *Boston Globe* has said: "Public television is no more elitist than the public library."

Rich or poor, most American homes do tune in to public television at least once a week. "Sesame

Street" opens the door, and so do family programs such as "Nature" and "Wonderworks Family Movie." In precable days, the Public Broadcasting Service, or PBS, was the only place to find such programs. During the 1980s PBS began to face competition from cable television. But even if cable TV reached every American home, PBS would still offer programs that can't be seen anywhere else.

The "serious" programs for which PBS is famous—such as "The MacNeil/Lehrer NewsHour," "Washington Week in Review," "Wall Street Week," or the cultural showcases "Masterpiece Theatre" and "Great Performances"—do not appeal to mass audiences. Yet, more than any other network, PBS needs viewers in order to survive, because its member stations rely directly on viewer dollars. So PBS has widened its scope. Under programming chief Jennifer Lawson, it is planning new comedies, dramas, talk shows, even game shows—but done in PBS style.

In an odd way, "Sesame Street" is a model for what PBS wants to attain in programs for children and adults. "Sesame Street" respects the curiosity and intelligence of its viewers. It also reflects a multi-ethnic world, both behind and in front of the camera. Lawson has promised that PBS will "embrace different cultures and races without catering to anyone." For instance, referring to the miniseries "Columbus and the Age of Discovery," which commemorated the 500th anniversary of Christopher Columbus's 1492 voyage to America, she said: "The question is, Was it a discovery to be celebrated or was it the beginning of an invasion of lands and the destruction of people?" And "Great Performances," the series that is often a showcase for high culture, has gone into urban streets to

Emmy Award–winner Wolfgang Bayer captures wildlife on film for many PBS and cable series, including "Nature" and "Nova."
The Best of Nature/Wolfgang Bayer Productions, Inc.

trace the musical roots of Madonna, Hammer, and other contemporary musicians.

No matter how it changes, public television is unlikely to become a clone of any other network. Its educational, noncommercial roots run deep.

"Learning channels" began to spring up in 1947, when WOI in Ames, Iowa, became the first instructional station in America. In 1951 the government set aside a group of channels for nonprofit educational use. FCC head Frieda Hennock crusaded for this as an antidote to television violence, which was already making people nervous. Congress approved the idea but didn't specify how to pay for it. Financing wasn't a problem at first, because most educational stations were shoestring operations run mainly for schools.

But by the mid-1960s half the country could get at least one public television station. Cable stations didn't exist yet, and people were hungry for something different from the standard fare on networks and local independent stations. Maybe educational television could provide something fresh and new. It was a grass-roots idea that recalled the nonprofit-TV movement of 1933, and it took hold. Congress created the Corporation for Public Broadcasting to set policies and channel funds, which came from the Ford Foundation (launched with the fortune earned by auto maker Henry Ford), businesses, government, and viewers themselves. PBS was set up in 1970 to distribute programming to its local member stations.

Excitement ran high in those first few years. Every night PBS presented programs that would never appear on commercial television—whole evenings of experimental and sometimes bizarre live theater, or gritty documentaries such as "None of My Business," about life on welfare. "The Great American Dream Machine," one of television's few successful ventures into satire, picked up where "Laugh-In" left off. It gave exposure to Jane Fonda and other stars who spoke out openly against the Vietnam War.

Not all early PBS programming was radical, of course. Some of the best programs, drawn from local stations, were anything but threatening: "Mister Rogers' Neighborhood" from Pittsburgh, "The French Chef with Julia Child" from Boston.

But President Richard M. Nixon, elected in 1968, was not amused that PBS sometimes bit the hand that fed it. Nixon vetoed its funding at every opportunity. According to broadcasting historian Erik Barnouw, he put PBS on a starvation diet.

PBS's dependence on government money has always been a problem. The original funding idea was to levy a small yearly fee on each set in the country, as England does. That would have allowed PBS to be self-sufficient. But the idea of "pay TV" in precable days was deadly, and PBS was left to fend for itself through a patchwork of sources.

PBS doesn't get all its money from on-air pledge drives, though they are so long and tedious it sometimes feels that way. Viewers provide only about one-fifth of its funding. Federal and state governments put in about a third. Most of the rest comes from corporations and colleges that sponsor programs. "Sesame Street" pays much of its own way through its licensing agreements.

PBS has been derisively called "Petroleum Broadcasting Service" and accused of selling out to corporate sponsors such as Mobil and other oil companies. When business foots the bill, critics say, the result is "safe" programming that is full of artistic merit but free of controversy.

PBS defenders say that corporate money—only about 16 percent of all funding—comes with no strings attached. They point to "American Playhouse," the main venue for work by American playwrights and screenwriters, and to landmark documentaries such as "Vietnam: A Television History" and "Eyes on the Prize," which discussed civil rights from a black perspective. "Masterpiece Theatre" even featured a fictional miniseries called "Traffik" that treated the drug trade like any other business. Those programs had corporate backing, and they were anything but bland.

Despite a chronic shortage of funds, at its best PBS blends education and entertainment better than any other network. With gems like the miniseries "The Civil War," it has reached huge audiences without compromising quality.

Cable television was supposed to usher in television's second golden age. Dozens of channels would provide room for every kind of program. Ratings would be less important and quality would soar. Minority voices would be heard, and public access channels would be open to anyone with something to say. Children's programs might even be commercial-free.

It has not worked out quite that way. Cable does offer more viewing choices, many of them good and outside the mainstream. But not many people watch or take part in public

"The Civil War," shown on PBS, was a television landmark. Creator Ken Burns combined interviews, music, letters, diaries, and archival photos to bring history to life.

Reproduced from the collections of the Library of Congress

access channels. And while cable does produce made-for-cable movies, original made-for-cable series are few and far between. For every program such as "Ray Bradbury Theater," there is also "Dog House" (about a talking dog), "Truck and Tractor Pull," and "The New Leave It to Beaver." And what does it say about cable audiences that the most-watched show on the most-watched cable channel (Turner Broadcasting System) has been "The Andy Griffith Show," which first aired in 1960?

Once an industry of mom-and-pop companies, cable is controlled by a few corporate giants, including Time Warner, Inc., Tele-Communications, Inc., and Viacom. They produce or syndicate many of the programs and own most of the systems that provide cable service to individual homes. The networks play a role, too. NBC owns CNBC/FNN and part of SportsChannel America, Bravo, and American Movie Classics. ABC owns most of ESPN and the Arts & Entertainment Network (A&E). CBS has negotiated with Turner on sports and, like NBC, subleased a portion of its Olympics coverage to TBS and other cable networks. Given that it has the same "parents" as mass entertainment and network television, how different can cable be?

No one dreamed that community access television—or CATV, as cable was first called—would grow into the multi-channel force it is today. CATV began as a simple wiring system. It was the only way for viewers in rural or mountainous areas to get television signals from the nearest big city.

In 1964 a group of businessmen and ex-network executives

Highly original cable programming: "Ray Bradbury Theater."
Photo courtesy of USA Network

tried an experiment, "subscription TV," in California. It was built around the baseball games of the Los Angeles Dodgers and San Francisco Giants. But the notion of pay television was unthinkable then, especially for major league sports, and the service never got off the ground.

A few years later Time Inc., a New York–based publisher, created Home Box Office. Like early television, HBO spotlighted Hollywood films, drama, boxing, and nightclub entertainment. Yet it was radically different—pay television without ads. HBO combined cable and satellite technology, and its range throughout the 1970s was fairly small. But it was the wave of the future.

At first competitors ran scared. Networks and owners of movie theaters used their clout to persuade the Federal Communications Commission to restrict this newcomer in the 1970s. More for cable—more ads, more channels, more viewers—might mean less for them. Yet entrepreneurs set up new cable ventures, and soon the networks did, too. Towns across America were being wired. Cable could not be stopped, and everyone knew it.

In 1980 the rules changed and the floodgates opened. Cable was free to compete with other broadcasters. The time was right: satellites had been perfected and were in place, offering the potential for dozens of channels. People had money to spend on entertainment, too. Advertisers were cautious but willing to try something new. Channels popped up almost overnight.

The most popular cable channels are those of general interest: Turner Broadcasting System, Turner Network Television, the USA Channel, and Nickelodeon. But some of the most interesting ones are the "narrowcast" channels: all arts, all news, all sports, all movies, all religious, all music, all business, all weather, all comedy.

At first, narrowcasting seemed risky. Who would watch one kind of programming around the clock? As it turned out, many people would. They also liked the freedom to dip into different kinds of programs whenever they wanted. With cable, viewers could become their own programmers, as long as they enjoyed what was offered.

Cable quickly moved to showcase the arts. CBS, ABC, and RCA (which then owned NBC) jumped in with ambitious channels of Golden Age caliber, two of which eventually merged to become A&E. Viewers willing to pay an extra monthly fee could tune in to Bravo for concerts and films that rivaled PBS offerings.

For information fiends, cable was a boon. The public had never seen the live daily workings of the U.S. Senate and House of Representatives until C-Span. And while the networks gave little time to financial news, cable had the Consumer News and Business Channel/Financial News Network, or CNBC/FNN.

At the other end of the business spectrum, cable made it possible to shop at home—at least for jewelry, furs, and household gadgets—using QVC, Home Shopping Network, and the JCPenney TV Shopping Channel. In a sense these channels are nothing but all-day advertisements. Fans don't seem to mind, as they buy over a billion dollars' worth of merchandise every year.

The all-music channels are basically twenty-four-hour advertisements, too, for groups and labels. But Music Television

(MTV), aimed at viewers up to age twenty-four, has added news, interviews, and game shows to its barrage of rock videos. MTV still prides itself on being "not normal TV" and proves it by giving away outrageous prizes that have included rock star Jon Bon Jovi's childhood home. Normal or not, MTV has become a cultural standard. Commercials for even the most mainstream products are often shot in rock-video style. Other cable channels imitate MTV: Video Hits-1 (the music channel for ages twenty-five to forty-nine, which is owned by MTV), Comedy Central, E! Entertainment Television, and the Nashville Network. None has done as well as MTV itself.

In 1984 the U.S. government freed cable operators to charge subscribers whatever the market would bear. That changed the sports scene. Higher fees gave ESPN, Sports-Channel America, and regional sports channels the money needed to negotiate for rights to major league sports. The hue and cry went up: *Americans won't pay to watch the Super Bowl!* But by 1987 half of America had cable—and the Super Bowl stayed on network television, so the hoopla died down.

Another ruckus arose when SportsChannel began to cover high-school sports, after two years of searching for sponsors. The fear was that national exposure and big-money sponsorships would corrupt schools and players. SportsChannel tried to avert this by giving attention to other aspects of athletics, such as marching bands, cheerleaders, and the athletes' grades.

To an extent, cable has broadened quality programming for young viewers. For families who can afford the premium fee, the Disney Channel offers a good selection of cartoons, movies, and specials without commercials. Nickelodeon could not remain ad-free, but its ad revenues help to create original daytime and weekend programming. The Discovery Channel and the Learning Channel serve up a wealth of geography and nature programs. Wild animals are often the stars here. "The bigger the beast, the better the ratings," quipped John S. Hendricks, founder of TDC.

Cable also helped to bring religion back to television. "Life Is Worth Living," starring Roman Catholic bishop Fulton Sheen, had been a prime-time presence in the 1950s, and there had always been a few religious shows on Sunday mornings. But on cable, ministers such as Jimmy Swaggart, Oral Roberts, Jerry Falwell, and Jim Bakker created their own electronic pulpits. Pat Robertson, former owner of the Christian Broadcasting Network and host of its "700 Club," capitalized on his fame to seek the Republican presidential nomination in 1988.

Some people deplored this programming as the commercialization of faith. Others welcomed it. The real issue wasn't religion itself but whether religious television would be dominated by the richest ministries.

With their newfound power to reach millions of viewers, "televangelists" could raise billions in donations. Some also succumbed to greed. Bakker was sentenced to forty-five years in prison for defrauding contributors, and his theme park and properties were sold in bankruptcy court. Swaggart left the air temporarily when his misdeeds were revealed. Roberts saw his donations drop after he said that God would "call him home" if he did not raise eight million dollars.

Despite the downfall of a few, televised religious programming seems here to stay. "When one minister fails, it doesn't alter [viewers'] basic faith; all they have to do is change the channel," said Jeffrey Hadden, a University of Virginia professor who has studied the phenomenon. "Christ told the apostles to teach to all nations," Archbishop John Foley, who was hired by Pope John Paul II in 1984 to bring coverage of the Roman Catholic Church to television news, told *Channels* magazine. "If Saint Paul were alive today, he'd be on television."

Evangelists now spread their message on a number of cable channels, including the New Inspirational Network and National Jewish Television. And the Christian Broadcasting Network has evolved into the Family Channel (TFC). It mixes religious programming with family shows that exclude sex and violence. TFC tries harder than other cable channels to create its own series, often using long-standing characters: "The New Zorro," "Rin Tin Tin K-9 Cop," and "The Black Stallion." It won new fans when it picked up "Beauty and the Beast" from CBS. However, a soap opera with moral overtones flopped.

Another cable channel that is intended to fulfill special needs is Black Entertainment Television. BET has something of interest for every age and taste: music videos, comedy, celebrity interviews, live concerts, public-affairs programs, profiles of black politicians, and even a special talk show for teenagers, "Teen Summit."

The networks were right to be scared of cable. It has eaten away at their audiences. Yet ABC, CBS, and NBC still pull about 60 percent of all prime-time viewers and are still the main source of original programs. And cable has problems of its own.

One of the biggest complaints to the FCC is that cable rates are too high and too quick to go up. Lawmakers have taken up the cause for the public. Cable executives have fought laws that would curb rates and regulate service, but they have worked from within to improve service. They have agreed to broadcast a variety of programming; to answer phone calls within thirty seconds; to install service to new customers within a week; and to restore lost service within twenty-four hours.

There are also more cable offerings than there are channels to show them, which is especially frustrating to consumers. Cable industry executives predict that new technologies will allow for as many as five hundred channels by the year 2000—but few cable systems currently have the space needed to offer the Cowboy TV Network, Court TV, and other new channels to their subscribers. Often the companies must drop one channel to make room for another, and they may lose fans of the old channel in the process.

USA Network's success with shows such as "Swamp Thing" led it to
buy the Sci-Fi Channel in 1992. Photo courtesy of USA Network

All the world loves cooking shows. The Spanish-language "Cocina Crisco" ("Crisco Kitchen") features ingredients made by its sponsor.
Photo courtesy of Univision

GOOD MORNING, WORLD:

International Television

Much of the world's television—almost half, by some counts—is made in America. The programs that travel best are the ones where the comedy is universal, or the drama is melodramatic. In France and Canada "Roseanne" and "Le Loi de Los Angeles" ("L.A. Law") have been hits. In Iceland and Yugoslavia "The Golden Girls" is a favorite. In Scandinavia and Germany "Cheers" lightens a schedule dominated by more serious offerings. Australians even try to solve "America's Unsolved Mysteries."

Unlike Americans, viewers elsewhere don't mind watching pro-

"It is the policy of Turner Broadcasting System that any person, event, etc., which is not part of the United States be referred to as *international* rather than *foreign*. The word *foreign* implies something unfamiliar and creates a perception of misunderstanding. In contrast, *international* means 'among nations' and promotes a sense of unity."
—Ted Turner, founder of Turner Broadcasting System

"American programs have good pacing, good decor, good actors, and European producers are trying to imitate them."
—Carlo Freccero, director of programming at the French station *La Cinq*

grams that are dubbed into their own language. And when television was still a novelty in very poor countries of Africa and Asia, many reruns were shown with no translation at all. "The story lines are quite easy to follow even if you know no English," said Kassaye Damena, former program director of Ethiopian Television. "My dad adored 'Bonanza' despite not being able to understand a word of it."

Yet American television has worn out its welcome in many countries. Canada and the European Community, especially, don't want U.S. culture to be the main one piped into their living rooms. They have quotas calling for at least half of all programs to be homegrown, even though American programs are often more popular and cheaper to import. To Jacques Delors, who heads the European Community group that voted for voluntary limits, the debate is territorial: "Culture is not a piece of merchandise. . . . I say to the U.S., 'Have we the right to exist, to perpetuate our own traditions?' "

To be sure, the world likes the U.S. *style* of television. From "Good Morning, Moscow" to "Australia's Funniest Home Videos," many foreign programs are clones of American shows. Lands as far-flung as Brazil and the Russian confederation even have CNN, ESPN, and MTV. European and South American producers often imitate shows such as "Dallas," but their creations have explicit language and scenes that would never be condoned on prime-time American television.

In most of the world—but not the United States—television is controlled by the government, and private channels are the exception. State-run channels do not have to answer to advertisers or corporate sponsors. Instead, they are funded by low yearly taxes on households with televisions. (Some also accept advertising but usually permit only a few hours of commercials each week.)

Governments in Europe do not usually interfere with state-run channels, but many other governments actively control what is broadcast. For decades, television news in the Soviet Union was pure propaganda—showing only what the government wanted people to see. South Africa has banned all news cameras for months at a time, so that the rest of the world could not see the government's savage treatment of blacks there. In the Philippines, former president Ferdinand Marcos denied television access to Corazon Aquino when she ran against him in the presidential election. Aquino got around him by putting her message onto videocassettes hand-delivered to voters, and she won. Even the United States has used television for political purposes, by beaming pro-American programs into nearby Communist Cuba.

Probably the world's most famous state-run network is the British Broadcasting Corporation. Its cultural programs are seen and heard around the world. The BBC gave the world "Monty Python's Flying Circus," the disturbing and odd "The Singing Detective," and "The Young Ones," a satire seen in the United States on MTV.

The same kind of mix can be found on Britain's commercial and satellite networks. They have produced everything from the high-brow "Brideshead Revisited," a thirteen-hour drama with exquisite acting by Sir Laurence Olivier and other stars, to "Heil Honey, I'm Home," a show about Adolf Hitler that was perhaps the world's most tasteless situation comedy. (Curiously, scenes of violence in "Miami Vice" have been edited for showing in the United Kingdom.) A quirk in British law helps decide what shows are imported there. No one under the age of sixteen can act on British series television because of child-labor laws, so Britons eat up American family programs such as "Roseanne," "The Waltons," and "Family Ties."

French television also has shows for every taste. Only in France has the host of a prime-time book-discussion program, Bernard Pivot of "Apostrophes," become a celebrity on the order of America's Phil Donahue. French viewers also love the few American programs that are permitted by quota and won't always accept homegrown substitutes. When "Dallas" swept the country, French producers quickly created "Chateauvallon," about a rich, feuding family much like the Ewings. It was 100 percent French (and far sexier than "Dallas"), but it didn't catch on.

Italian television is intertwined with politics. The private networks are controlled by political parties—one by the Christian Democrats, one by the Communists, and one by Socialists. The bias of each can be seen in the news and in debates. Most Italians turn to "Telegiornale," on one of the state-run channels, for nightly news. There they see *all* political points of view, sometimes presented by as many as six anchors at once.

Unlike Italy, Germany tries hard *not* to mix politics and broadcasting. Germans want to avoid repeating the mistakes of the 1930s, when Adolf Hitler's skillful use of the mass media helped him rise to power. So while Germany's networks are state-run and subsidized by commercials, they are regional—and no single region or advertiser has too much power. One result is a lack of national television "stars." Instead there is a little bit of everything: drama and classical music, real-life crime shows (Germany invented the genre in the 1960s with "File on XY . . . Unsolved"), even movies by Andy Warhol and other avant-garde artists rarely seen on television elsewhere. Commercials are banned on prime time and on Sundays.

One oddity of German television is that programs of the same type are not allowed to run at the same time, so German viewers always have distinct choices. However, the networks may make the choice for them. If major news is breaking, live coverage may replace all regular programs. While this happened for days when the Berlin Wall fell and when East and West Germany were reunified, no one complained about missing their favorite shows.

It can be hard to find the programs amid the commercials in Mexico, Brazil, and the countries of Central and South America. On Latin American television, ads may pop up every three or four minutes. American television seems uninterrupted by comparison.

Between commercials, the Latin American networks focus on entertainment and sports. Most popular are the *telenovelas*, a kind of soap opera. Each has basically the same plot: a poor but pretty young woman travels to a big city,

"Sabado Gigante," with host Don Francisco, who is as popular with Hispanic audiences as Johnny Carson was with Americans.
Photo courtesy of Univision

works as a maid or shop clerk, meets a handsome man, and prospers in marriage, motherhood, or career. (One variation has been to make the main character a young man who meets a beautiful young woman.) Prime-time *telenovelas* are often seen six nights a week.

Variety shows like "Sabado Gigante" (Gigantic Saturday) and "Feliz Domingo" ("Happy Sunday") are another trademark of Latin American television. Up to twelve hours long, they provide a backdrop of games, raffles, singing, dancing, quizzes, and animal acts, as viewers go about their weekend tasks. Almost anything can happen: sometimes the station owner strolls onto the set, holds up his hand to the camera, and begins telling stories. One such program was hosted by Silvio Santos, who owned the network on which he appeared. He became a star and used his popularity to run for president of Brazil. And in Cuba, one of the few Latin American countries with a state-run channel, dictator Fidel Castro has often preempted regular programming to talk for hours at a time. On those nights, Castro himself is the prime-time show.

The networks of Mexico and Brazil, which supply programs to all of Latin America as well as Spain and Portugal, have been accused of racism. Many of their news teams and actors do not look native; they are blond and blue-eyed. Joaquin Blaya, president of Mexico's Univision network, shrugs off the criticism: "Television as well as movies is a business for beautiful people. It's entertainment." Xuxa, a young, blond Brazilian celebrity who hosts a children's program with an all-blond cast, adds: "Children like Snow White, Cinderella, Barbie. When they see me . . . it's as if the mythical person has become reality."

Canada faced a different identity problem. So many of its programs came from the United States, Britain, and France that the government demanded "Canadian content" in half of all shows. That brought new *teleromans* (French-speaking cousins of *telenovelas*) set in Montreal and Vancouver, MTV-like channels in English and French, and community programs on cable. But millions of Canadians near the southern border still watch U.S. stations, despite a full range of domestic channels and the state-run Canadian Broadcasting Corporation.

Japan was also worried that its culture would be destroyed by foreign television. And the Japanese watch more television than almost anyone, even more than do Americans. So the country simply stopped importing programs in the 1960s. Television is now the main stage for Japan's traditional Kabuki plays and bunraku puppet shows. Ancient legends get new life in programs such as "Samurai Executioner," which are far more violent than American crime programs. Japan also produces a lavish and patriotic historical drama every year, with new episodes each Sunday night. The setting of this series often become the year's hottest tourist attraction.

However, Japanese television does borrow from the rest of the world. Children have their own version of "Sesame Street," and adults have a clone of "Entertainment Tonight," hosted by Sachi Parker, the Japanese-speaking daughter of actress Shirley MacLaine. There is more news from the United States since NBC and CBS joined with Japanese broadcasters to create satellite-news organizations. And Japan's Nippon

Samurai dramas are a staple of Japanese prime time. They are often quite violent. Photo courtesy of NHK

Japanese television often mixes the modern and the historical.
Photo courtesy of NHK

Television Network even paid $4 million to restore the Sistine Chapel in Rome, with its treasures by Michelangelo, partly so it could film the proceedings and turn them into television specials.

Israel is another country that feared the changes television might bring. It held out against all forms of television except classroom programs until 1967 but finally realized it was fighting a losing battle. Israelis were buying sets at inflated prices on the black market to watch channels from Jordan and other nearby countries. A state channel gave them their own news and consumer programs, with entertainment in the evenings only. The other countries of the Middle East have freer schedules, often showing dramas and comedies produced in Egypt, which is the Hollywood of the region.

South Africans fought television longer than anyone. For a country mired in racial separatism, not having television was another way of keeping the modern world at bay. Officials called television the "evil black box" and feared its introduction would bring American-style materialism, Communism, or images of a better life for blacks. When the country finally changed its mind in 1976, South African screens echoed the apartheid system: separate channels for whites and blacks, all under tight control by the state. Many blacks there still cannot afford television sets, but they watch anyway, in bars or at the homes of friends. They can also pick up nonapartheid channels from across the country's borders.

In Third World nations—those struggling toward modernization—television has been a low priority for other reasons. Radio is cheaper and reaches more people. Language is also a barrier in countries such as China and India, where many people speak local dialects, not the official national language used on television.

Yet most poor countries have instructional television programs, often viewed at "teleclubs" in schools or community centers by those who cannot afford their own sets. In India, people have learned how to plant more productive crops, to avoid disease, and even how to read and write by watching such programs. In Africa's Ivory Coast, educators used instructional television to help them teach almost every subject, and the nation has a much higher literacy rate (35 percent) than neighboring countries.

Once instructional television takes hold, entertainment programs are usually not far behind. In Third World countries, prime-time lineups once consisted mainly of third-rate American Westerns and thrillers. But slowly the emerging countries of Africa, Asia, and South Africa are producing their own news, talk shows, and homegrown sitcoms.

The People's Republic of China is a special case. Many of its people still lack the money and electricity needed for television. Yet it has the world's largest audience, with up to ten viewers for each of the country's 65 million sets. They get a steady diet of propaganda on the main state-run network. But in matters other than politics, the government is slowly allowing some leeway. "One World with Yue-Sai Kan," an American-style documentary in English and Mandarin Chinese, has taken its viewers to England, Paris, and the ethnic neighborhoods of New York City. The city government of Beijing has even acted as a television matchmaker on "Tonight We Meet," a new twist on China's tradition of arranged marriages.

Television was also a window on the world for the former Soviet Union. For decades Russian television was state-run and stodgy, with only an occasional gangster series or soap opera from Europe to enliven it. But *glasnost*, the policy of openness that began in the 1980s, brought changes. A few programs allowed citizens to phone in their opinions and hear discussions freely critical of the government. They could even tune into two of America's most democratic exports: MTV and PBS's "Adam Smith's Money World," dubbed in Russian and sponsored by "capitalist" corporations such as AT&T and General Motors. And by 1991, when Communist Party rule toppled, the national television news was no longer a government whitewash.

A late-night program called "600 Seconds," described by its host, Aleksandr Nevzorov, as "information shock," is a good example of the new Russian television. As a big digital clock counts down the seconds, Nevzorov hyperactively narrates a montage of daily events that might include crime news, environmental horrors, and consumer ripoffs. In one show, a story about a radioactive zucchini was followed by an official tribute to Air Force Day. And while other news programs invited economists to talk about the country's shortage of soap, "600 Seconds" interviewed a woman who had been forced to wash with an elegant soap sculpture that her family had treasured for decades.

Television has brought American programs and ideas to the rest of the world. It is ironic, then, that American television rarely looks beyond its own borders. UHF stations in bigger cities do carry native-language programs for immigrant viewers—often Korean, Japanese, Polish, Italian, Indian, or Greek—but these are almost never translated into English. Neither are the programs on Telemundo, Univision, or Galavision, America's Spanish-language networks. Those who watch PBS or the more serious cable networks will see a handful of imports, mostly British series and foreign movies.

The production of American television is becoming more global. For financial reasons, many made-for-TV movies and miniseries, such as "Young Catherine," a biography of Catherine the Great, are joint ventures with producers from Britain or Europe. These are often filmed abroad; they look lavish and exotic. But they do not give a feeling for what it's like to live in another culture.

Aside from "CNN World Report" (a short weekly program of news produced abroad) and the "DeGrassi Street" series from Canada, the United States has had no regularly scheduled programs that are not made here. And until it does, Americans will miss out on one of the best things television can offer: a sense of how other people live.

THE BOOB TUBE:

The Case Against Television

One of the earliest mass-produced television sets in America, made by the Pilot Radio Corporation, looked like a bank safe. The screen sat behind heavy doors that could be locked shut. The idea was that if this new machine proved *too* alluring, if it seemed to hold the family under its spell, parents could bolt up the set and hide the key. The set didn't sell.

Some people would still like to put a lock on television. Their reasons are familiar. Television is violent. It's boring. It traffics in dumb situations and easy laughs. It stereotypes everyone. It turns viewers

"Well, gentlemen, you seem to have perfected the greatest time waster of all mankind. I hope you use it well."
—Isaac Schoenberg, engineer involved with television in the 1920s

"Television would be wonderful if it were only on Wednesday nights."
—Grant Tinker, former CBS executive and former head of MTM Productions

into "vidiots" with short attention spans. It's cluttered with ads that urge people to buy things they don't need. Even avid fans must admit that these arguments contain a grain of truth, and sometimes more.

Most people turn on the set to relax, but regular viewing makes viewers *more* tense. We are absorbed yet restless at the same time, because television rarely challenges the mind. These results have been charted in studies of more than 1,100 viewers. They are also well known to anyone who has felt fidgety, grouchy, or unfocused after a few hours in front of the set.

Television can also overload us with images. When floods, earthquakes, and shootings constantly flicker past our eyes, they stop seeming real. We can lose interest in the outside world. In studies done in 1990, people aged eighteen to twenty-nine who watched an average amount of television— about six hours a day—said they didn't care much about public affairs. They knew less and voted less than people their age had done in the past. These findings do suggest that young adults aren't being brainwashed by political ads on television. But they are also turning off to issues that affect their lives, such as taxes, pollution, and war.

As bad as television can be for adults, it can be infinitely worse for children, who are a captive audience. Kids don't have as many programs to choose from, good or bad. Some people even claim that the very act of watching television is harmful to young viewers, no matter if they're tuned into "Sesame Street" or "G.I. Joe."

In her landmark book *The Plug-In Drug*, Marie Winn argued that television causes a changed state of consciousness

Highly political miniseries like "Amerika," which drew protests at
the ABC studios in New York, have become extinct on network television. AP/Wide World Photos

in children. Young viewers watch as if in a trance, she said, and afterward they are irritable and wound up. Winn also argued that the television habit keeps kids from reading, writing, and playing.

Arguments like these aren't always scientific. After all, as Winn herself noted, it isn't possible to dissect the brains of living children to see if television has altered them. We can only observe the effects. It's been proved that school-age children who watch a lot have lower achievement scores. But is television itself to blame for these effects, or does the fault lie with parents who overuse it as a baby-sitter?

Also, because it's everywhere, television is an easy scapegoat for many of society's ills. Yet much of what is blamed on television might also be blamed on movies, radio, magazines, and other parts of American culture.

The danger may not be too much television but too little attention from parents or other adults. At least that's what a Yale University experiment has suggested.

It involved four groups of preschoolers and "Mister Rogers' Neighborhood." The first group watched the program by themselves every day for two weeks. The second group watched it with adults, who talked to them about the program and did activities based on it. The third group watched no television at all but got special attention from adults for an hour every day. The fourth group didn't watch any television either but didn't get any special adult attention.

At the end of the two weeks, it was the third group—the nonviewers who got special attention—who showed the most growth in creativity and imaginative play. The group that watched "Mister Rogers' Neighborhood" with adults also did well. The two groups with no adult interaction did worst.

One fact, easier to measure, can't be argued. The more television that children watch, the less they exercise—and the fatter they tend to be. That's one reason the American Academy of Pediatrics urges parents to limit the hours that kids watch.

Each year thousands of murders, shootings, rapes, and fights are played out on the television screen. The influence of television is often blamed for increases in violent crimes. But despite hundreds of studies, no one really knows if there are actual connections between what people watch and what they do.

To be sure, some studies have found links. For instance, the American Academy of Pediatrics says that while television-watching doesn't *make* children become bossy or pick fights, it can aggravate such behavior. Again, adult involvement makes a big difference. Those children who act most aggressively after watching television tend to live in homes where parents are not around or where domestic violence goes unchecked.

Spurred on by rising crime or voter disgust, even the U.S. Congress and Surgeon General have tackled the question of television violence many times. The results are usually the same: the government urges less violence on television but leaves it up to broadcasters to police themselves.

The response has been lukewarm, mainly because those in the television industry hate being told what to do. To them, a

quota on violence would border on censorship. And if violence is an audience-pleaser—which it often is—no network
wants to lose out. (Marie Winn believes that viewers choose
violence because they want a *feeling* of activity while they sit
safely and passively at home.) In 1989, when the U.S. House
of Representatives asked broadcasters for voluntary limits on
television violence, CBS vice president Martin D. Franks
spoke out against the request. "The bottom line is that consumers vote on our programming several times every night
when they hit their remote-control button," Franks told the
New York Times. "The best way to get [violence] off is not to
watch it."

Networks set limits on "unacceptable" violence, but their
guidelines sometimes make little sense. At one time it was
allowable to show a gun, then to show a head, but not to show
the gun *to* the head. Similar rules still apply to children's
programs, where they can become absurd. The idea is to
shelter young viewers from cruel realities, but how real is it
when one of G.I. Joe's soldiers takes a blow to the arm (never
to the heart) and doesn't bleed or die? Real violence hurts
and kills—but never on Saturday-morning cartoons.

To the credit of the industry, television violence has been
on the decline. Yet in the early 1990s, according to the
National Coalition on TV Violence, about 30 percent of
programs still glamorized or promoted it.

The American Academy of Pediatrics believes the television
industry should portray sex more responsibly as well, especially in this age of AIDS. Watching an average of twenty-
three hours of television and video every week, viewers aged
twelve to eighteen hear sex mentioned about 14,000 times a

To some viewers, "The A-Team" was television at its worst. It was violent—although even the bad guys rarely bled. It stereotyped black men as macho menaces—although the hero, B.A. (played by Mr. T, at left), also helped victims of bigotry. It was a huge success.
AP/Wide World Photos

year. Only about 150 of those innuendos refer to responsible sex, contraception, or abstinence.

Another gripe about television is that it exists only to sell. Of course, that's part of the territory, because commercial television is a business. And viewers are not forced to watch commercials, to buy what is advertised, or to buy the merchandise based on television programs. But it's hard not to be swayed by television culture, and it's especially hard for younger viewers. In *Selling America's Kids: Commercial Pressures on Kids of the 90's,* the Consumers Union's Educational Services Division described a day in the life of an American child:

> It's 7 a.m. as America's kid awakens on Ninja Turtle sheets. He rises, dons Superman underwear, a Dick Tracy T-shirt, and sits down to Nintendo breakfast cereal with his Simpsons bookbag beside him. His sister downs her pink Breakfast With Barbie cereal, ready to pick up her Garfield notebook and catch the school bus.

Furthermore, many parents and critics believe that children are manipulated by the sales pitches of cereal, candy, and toy manufacturers. They argue that it isn't fair to target people too young to assess advertising claims.

As *Selling America's Kids* explains: "The hook is affection—for a favorite show, movie, character. The goal is a purchase. The target is a child. The problem is the pressure to purchase, over and over again, as new shows, movies, characters win their affection." Nickelodeon Club, Fox Kids Club, Disney's Mickey Mouse Club, and the MTV Record Club are also culprits. "In a real club, kids are likely to find friends, shared interests and activities. . . . [But] the only way to participate in the [kids'] clubs we join is to buy things," said the report.

Kids' clubs date back to the radio days of the 1930s, but high-pressure merchandising aimed at kids has grown far more sophisticated over the years. One landmark was Mattel's first filmed ad for a toy, the Mattel Burp Gun, in 1955. The gun sold out immediately; even President Dwight D. Eisenhower had to call Mattel to find one as a Christmas gift for his young grandson. Other toy manufacturers jumped on the bandwagon. Mattel itself struck everlasting gold with Barbie, which it advertised on television not as a doll but as a teen model. When Barbie was market-tested, almost 100 percent of mothers hated it. They said the doll was too sophisticated, too much of a sex symbol. But almost 100 percent of young girls loved Barbie, and they prevailed.

In the United States alone, preteens have a say in the purchase of eight billion dollars worth of goods each year. So they are the target of commercials for products other than the usual toys, vitamins, and cereals. Even the Boy Scouts of America uses television to promote membership, spending a million dollars on MTV-like ads that invite viewers to "join the Scouts and chill out."

The advertising agencies that create toy and cereal commercials insist that children are smarter than adults give them credit for. Toy makers warn that without commercials there would be no non-PBS programming for children at all, and they are right. In *Selling America's Kids*, Consumers Union suggests one remedy to cries of viewer manipulation: "Promotions that target kids must meet higher standards than those aimed at adults. They should not exploit the inexperience and vulnerabilities of kids, and they should clearly identify themselves as advertising."

The debate over commercialism and television spread to classrooms in the 1990s. It fueled an argument against Whittle Communications's "Channel One," a daily news program for junior and senior high-school students that contained ten minutes of news and two minutes of commercials.

Few people faulted "Channel One" on its news coverage. It reported on international events and topics with student appeal, such as the lives of black teenagers in racially divided South Africa or the real odds (one in 3,279) on a high-school basketball star turning pro. Schools liked the opportunity to receive free televisions and satellite receivers for as long as they subscribed. And while most of the commercials were for products such as Nike sneakers and Pepsi, some had a noncommercial message. For example, Burger King ran ads that urged viewers not to drop out of school.

Yet for many, two minutes of ads was too high a price to pay. In refusing to take part in "Channel One," PBS issued this statement: "School is a marketplace for ideas, not products. The minds of our children are not for sale." California, New York, and Rhode Island forbade "Channel One" in public schools. Other educators felt the battle against commercialization in America had long been lost. If this program would improve students' knowledge of the world, they reasoned, it was worth trying.

"CNN Newsroom" gave "Channel One" competition without commercials. Except for daily teachers' guides that cost a dollar, it, too, was free, although schools had to provide their own cable hookups and television sets. Some schools preferred "CNN Newsroom" because it was longer (fifteen minutes) and didn't try as hard as "Channel One" to be entertaining. An early look at both classroom newscasts showed that, with or without commercials, they worked well only if teachers used them as a starting point for discussion of the issues covered.

Many classrooms are still free of television, but only a few households do without it. Fewer than 2 percent of Americans don't watch at all; they have no time or no interest.

From time to time, families or communities that feel dominated by television will sample life without it—often following the guidelines offered in Marie Winn's book *Unplugging the Plug-in Drug.* No-TV experiments, lasting a week or a month, have taken place in Denver, Colorado, Providence, Rhode Island, and other cities. The results have been similar.

In most cases, preschoolers have barely noticed the lack of television. It's the older children who have missed it most. Without their favorite programs, they have felt "lost" or out of touch with their friends. In one month-long experiment, the first week was especially hard for children under twelve because without television they didn't know what day it was.

Adults were usually the ones who instigated these television-free periods, but they discovered a drawback, too. They lost one of their most effective methods of discipline: the threat of "no TV." And the adults who stayed home on weekdays missed the "companionship" that television can provide.

But on the whole, both adults and young people who gave up television for a brief while reported good results: more interaction and closeness between children and parents, a more peaceful home, and longer and more relaxed mealtimes. Children helped more with chores, played outside more, read more, took part in other activities, and went to bed earlier.

But for many people, the question is not how to live without television but how to balance it with other parts of life. The former advocacy group Action for Children's Television had some good ideas for parents and children who feel that television is cutting into family time. ACT urged families to watch together as much as possible and to talk about what they see. It's also a good idea, they said, to learn more about the industry, to keep track of likes and dislikes, and to let networks and advertisers know how you feel. "And use the VCR to tape and rent better programs," ACT founder Peggy Charren has said. "Television is whatever comes across on the screen. With the VCR, we have much more control."

As does the American Academy of Pediatrics, ACT suggested that children watch for no more than two hours per day. "You have the power and obligation to improve your family's viewing habits," Charren insists.

INTO THE TWENTY-FIRST CENTURY:

The Future of Television

In a classic episode of "The Honeymooners," Ralph Kramden didn't want to buy his first television set. The reason, he said, was that black-and-white sets would soon be replaced by three-dimensional television.

Somewhere in rerun land, Ralph still waits for his "3-D TV." But his general prediction was right. Black-and-white television *has* been superseded—by color television, cable, VCRs, and home video. Technology will bring even more changes in the twenty-first century.

Each year, new television sets look different. They become bigger and flatter, more like movie screens

> "The TV satellite is going to blanket the whole world with all sorts of information. . . . I call it the 'electronic nervous system of all mankind.' Within a lifetime, it will be possible for anyone to talk to anybody."
> —Arthur C. Clarke, futurist and science-fiction author

and less like boxes. The image quality is brighter, sharper, and more movielike, too. Andy Lippman, associate director of the New Media Lab at the Massachusetts Institute of Technology (MIT), says we are evolving toward a flat screen that is perhaps two inches thick and will hang on a wall. The second (or third, or fourth) set in the household may be a projection system that has no screen at all but that beams onto any wall.

As screens get bigger, it becomes impossible to ignore them. Watching one is like walking into a scene or being on a playing field. Or course, those who might feel swallowed up by life-sized images will still be able to find smaller sets. Indeed, they will probably be able to buy wristwatch TVs that pick up satellite signals.

In the twenty-first century, high-definition television, or HDTV, will be the norm. Picture quality is twice as good with HDTV systems, but changes can't be made overnight.

The problem is that the channel system set up fifty years ago is finally becoming obsolete. Current channels don't have enough space to carry the extra electronic information needed for HDTV. Western Europe and Japan decided on a satellite-based system and quickly made the technical changes needed to introduce HDTV. The U.S. government has taken longer, partly because it insisted on a ground-based system instead of satellites. It didn't want American consumers to have to buy satellite dishes to pick up HDTV signals.

Just as some programs ("Superman" is one) were filmed in color before color television became the norm, some shows of the 1990s (such as "Cheers") are being filmed in high definition. When HDTV is widespread, they will be more marketable as reruns.

The action is life-sized when viewers can adjust the size of the pic-
ture up to 100 diagonal inches. Shown here is SharpVision
XV120ZU, which plugs into any television set, VCR, laser disc player,
Camcorder, or video game. It projects images onto a screen or wall.
Photo courtesy of Sharp Electronics Corporation

Viewers will have to own HDTV sets to receive HDTV. And those who want to be the first ones on the block with HDTV will pay five-digit sums, although the current astronomical price of HDTV sets will probably drop. A more affordable upgrade is extended-definition television, or EDTV, which sharpens detail and eliminates ghosts. For many viewers, EDTV is good enough—especially when combined with high-end features such as stereo sound, screens within screens (to watch two or more channels at once), and the ability to zoom, pan, and freeze images.

Engineers are even working on televisions that respond to voice commands. Those in the MIT Media Lab say that viewers will soon be able to tell their set to turn itself off or to change channels. Remote controls may become a thing of the past.

And instead of reading the daily television listings, people may turn that task over to advanced VCRs. Viewers can electronically check off the types of shows they like to watch: perhaps baseball playoffs, reruns of "Murphy Brown," or all programs about bears. The "genius VCR" then searches each day's offerings and automatically records the viewer's preferences. Prototypes of this system even present an on-screen menu with a brief description of each show.

Another possibility is that television sets of the future will actually be computers that can pick up television signals. These computers may also tie into the home telephone, modem, and facsimile machine and to computer bulletin boards and libraries. In effect, ordinary households may be linked to a global network, as futurists have predicted for decades. But it's more likely that viewers will use such megamachines to order in a pizza and a movie—or to watch television and do homework at the same time on split screens.

Scenarios like these will happen only when the lines between telephone and television are blurred. Telephone companies have developed "information highways" made of optical fibers that can transmit one thousand times more data than copper wire does. They have lobbied for new regulations so that they can transmit visual images as well as voice. The potential exists for hundreds of two-way channels.

New technology is inevitable. But how much change can we expect in what we *see* on our big screens or our television-computer terminals? Probably not much.

Television may become more interactive. In recent tests, viewers could change camera angles as they watched sports or concerts. They could play along with game shows, vote for the outcome of a mystery, pick the music video they wanted to see, or select an exercise session according to how hard or easy it was. This doesn't mean anyone on the other end was really listening. All the "choices" were prerecorded.

Interactive programming has been slow to catch on, partly because cable systems haven't had the extra channels needed to offer it. Maybe it's also because this programming is more gimmicky than new. Many people watch television in order *not* to interact. And knowing what happens next in a story always ruins the surprise.

An experiment in interactive television failed in the 1970s. Qube, installed in Columbus, Ohio, was the first interactive channel. Viewers pushed buttons to offer their opinions on

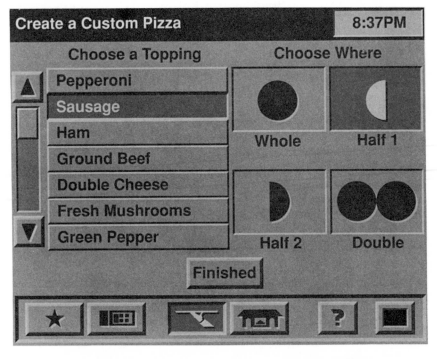

One item on the interactive television menu. Others are sports, game shows, home banking, home shopping, and access to electronic libraries.
Screen simulated photo courtesy of TV Answer, Inc.

the day's events or to pick the winners of political debates. Qube was a novelty at a time when cable operators were competing for the right to wire cities and towns; big money was at stake, and it looked good to offer the promise of a channel "by the people and for the people." But because viewers' responses went into a databank, some people saw Qube as an invasion of privacy. The people of Columbus simply got bored with it, and Qube quietly faded in 1984.

Direct-broadcast satellite (DBS) systems have also been called a new force in television, because they broadcast by satellite and thus bypass network and cable altogether. But with networks and cable companies owning huge stakes in DBS systems, DBS is unlikely to bring new programming. Four-channel Sky Television in Britain and Europe was the first big satellite network, but its programs were hardly in-novative. On one typical evening, it offered England's annual Trades Union Congress, Bulgarian women's volleyball, a talk show about marriage, and an old Hollywood film.

Even in Europe, where viewers are much quicker than Americans to adopt new technologies, the market couldn't support two DBS networks. Sky merged with its chief com-petitor to become British Sky Broadcasting. The same shake-out may happen when satellite takes hold in the United States. How many channels can programmers fill and viewers watch (or even tape)?

Yet new channels are on the horizon. Fred Silverman and other industry insiders predict that Disney, Paramount, or other movie studios may create a fifth broadcast network to compete with ABC, CBS, NBC, and Fox—or even that the studios may buy the networks. Cable systems are investing millions to add channel capacity that will make room for new cable offerings. And at the other end of the spectrum there is something truly new: low-power stations. They were invented in the 1980s, when the Federal Communications Commission decided that very small, inexpensive stations—those with a twenty-five-mile or less reach—were needed to balance the networks and independent stations. By the year 2000, about four thousand low-power stations will exist on VHF, UHF, and cable systems.

Some low-power stations are full of cheap reruns, but others are truly local. Nebraska viewers can watch the country's first all-rural channel, RFD-TV in Omaha. Parents in and around Hopkinsville, Kentucky, can tape their children's high-school graduation by setting their VCR to TV43. In Los Angeles, the low-power Silent Network has a full range of captioned programs for the deaf. Consumer advocate Ralph Nader helped set up Buffalo's low-power station; it carries local government meetings, like a mini-C-Span.

Another real change may be the growth of specialized networks for groups such as doctors and lawyers. School districts are also banding together to create their own networks as a way to save classes that may otherwise fall victim to low enrollments and high costs. And more live trials will probably be seen on television, in federal as well as state courts.

But true changes in everyday television will probably be scarce. The national news on the networks may look different, relying less on the star anchor and more on input from stations around the country. "For example, Peter Jennings's co-anchor may be every local anchor in America," says Don Hewitt. Or national news may be totally absorbed into local news, with the anchor doing brief segments that are slotted in as "The Rather Report" or "The Koppel Update."

On the entertainment front, one-hour dramas may become rarer because their rerun rights have been harder to sell. Reality-based programs such as "America's Funniest Home Videos" may proliferate, even when people tire of them, because they are cheap to produce. On the other hand, as more and more channels compete for the same number of viewers, programmers may be more willing to take chances. That may mean more programs by serious film directors—and also more programs with mindless shock value.

Good or bad, new programs may hang on longer. "It costs millions to cancel a show," said Fred Silverman. "Networks have more patience now. If a show is halfway decent, they'll let audiences build."

One thing is clear: in the twenty-first century, television will be bigger than ever. Larger sets will take up more space in our homes. New channels will make more demands on our time.

With so much television to choose from, viewers will have to become more selective. That isn't hard to do. CBS's Don Hewitt puts the task into perspective.

"People expect too much of television," said Hewitt flatly, at a time when his "60 Minutes" was the top-rated program. "Let's say you pay five hundred dollars for a set and it lasts five years. Maybe television has taken you to the Olympics or the Super Bowl. It's given you the news and weather whenever you want it. Maybe you're into musical opera or soap opera. Everybody's got a few favorite sitcoms. Add it up. You can't expect a hundred dollars' worth of television enjoyment every night, but haven't you gotten a hundred dollars' worth every year?"

Without expecting miracles from the television industry, we *can* demand much more of it—and much more of ourselves as viewers.

APPENDIX 1   TOP-RATED PRIME-TIME PROGRAMS

(The three most-watched prime-time shows each season, based on ratings from the A. C. Nielsen Company)

1950–1951
"Texaco Star Theater," "Fireside Theater," "Philco TV Playhouse"
1951–1952
"Arthur Godfrey's Talent Scouts," "Texaco Star Theater," "I Love Lucy"
1952–1953
"I Love Lucy," "Arthur Godfrey's Talent Scouts," "Arthur Godfrey and His Friends"
1953–1954
"I Love Lucy," "Dragnet," "Arthur Godfrey's Talent Scouts"
1954–1955
"I Love Lucy," "The Jackie Gleason Show," "Dragnet"
1955–1956
"The $64,000 Question," "I Love Lucy," "The Ed Sullivan Show"
1956–1957
"I Love Lucy," "The Ed Sullivan Show," "General Electric Theater"
1957–1958
"Gunsmoke," "The Danny Thomas Show," "Tales of Wells Fargo"
1958–1959
"Gunsmoke," "Wagon Train," "Have Gun Will Travel"
1959–1960
"Gunsmoke," "Wagon Train," "Have Gun Will Travel"
1960–1961
"Gunsmoke," "Wagon Train," "Have Gun Will Travel"
1961–1962
"Wagon Train," "Bonanza," "Gunsmoke"
1962–1963
"The Beverly Hillbillies," "Candid Camera," "The Red Skelton Show"
1963–1964
"The Beverly Hillbillies," "Bonanza," "The Dick Van Dyke Show"

1964–1965
"Bonanza," "Bewitched," "Gomer Pyle, U.S.M.C."
1965–1966
"Bonanza," "Gomer Pyle, U.S.M.C.," "The Lucy Show"
1966–1967
"Bonanza," "The Red Skelton Hour," "The Andy Griffith Show"
1967–1968
"The Andy Griffith Show," "The Lucy Show," "Gomer Pyle, U.S.M.C."
1968–1969
"Rowan & Martin's Laugh-In," "Gomer Pyle, U.S.M.C.," "Bonanza"
1969–1970
"Rowan & Martin's Laugh-In," "Gunsmoke," "Bonanza"
1970–1971
"Marcus Welby, M.D.," "The Flip Wilson Show," "Here's Lucy"
1971–1972
"All in the Family," "The Flip Wilson Show," "Marcus Welby, M.D."
1972–1973
"All in the Family," "Sanford and Son," "Hawaii Five-O"
1973–1974
"All in the Family," "The Waltons," "Sanford and Son"
1974–1975
"All in the Family," "Sanford and Son," "Chico and the Man"
1975–1976
"All in the Family," "Rich Man, Poor Man," "Laverne & Shirley"
1976–1977
"Happy Days," "Laverne & Shirley," "ABC Monday Night Movie"
1977–1978
"Laverne & Shirley," "Happy Days," "Three's Company"
1978–1979
"Laverne & Shirley," "Three's Company," "Mork & Mindy" and "Happy
    Days" (tied for third place)
1979–1980
"60 Minutes," "Three's Company," "That's Incredible"
1980–1981
"Dallas," "The Dukes of Hazzard," "60 Minutes"

1981–1982

"Dallas," "60 Minutes," "The Jeffersons"

1982–1983

"60 Minutes," "Dallas," "M*A*S*H" and "Magnum, P.I." (tied for third place)

1983–1984

"Dallas," "60 Minutes," "Dynasty"

1984–1985

"Dynasty," "Dallas," "The Cosby Show"

1985–1986

"The Cosby Show," "Family Ties," "Murder, She Wrote"

1986–1987

"The Cosby Show," "Family Ties," "Cheers"

1987–1988

"The Cosby Show," "A Different World," "Cheers"

1988–1989

"The Cosby Show," "Roseanne," "A Different World"

1989–1990

"Roseanne," "The Cosby Show," "Cheers"

1990–1991

"Cheers," "60 Minutes," "Roseanne"

1991–1992

"60 Minutes," "Roseanne," "Murphy Brown"

∿∿

The Emmy Awards are television's top awards. They are given by the National Academy of Television Arts and Sciences to over-the-air programs. (The cable industry has its own ACE Awards.)

Dozens of Emmy Awards are presented each year, for excellence in perform-ance and production. Here is a very abbreviated list of winners.

1948
Best Film Made for Television: "The Necklace" ("Your Show Time") (NBC)

1949
Best Live Show: "The Ed Wynn Show" (CBS)
Best Kinescope Show: "Texaco Star Theater" (NBC)

1950
Best Dramatic Show: "Pulitzer Prize Playhouse" (ABC)
Best Variety Show: "The Alan Young Show" (CBS)

1951
Best Dramatic Show: "Studio One" (CBS)
Best Variety Show: "Your Show of Shows" (NBC)
Best Comedy Show: "The Red Skelton Show" (CBS)

1952
Best Dramatic Program: "Robert Montgomery Presents" (NBC)
Best Variety Program: "Your Show of Shows" (NBC)
Best Situation Comedy: "I Love Lucy" (CBS)

1953
Best Dramatic Program: "The U.S. Steel Hour" (ABC)
Best Variety Program: "Omnibus" (CBS)
Best Situation Comedy: "I Love Lucy" (CBS)

1954
Best Dramatic Series: "The U.S. Steel Hour" (ABC)
Best Variety Series Including Musical Varieties: "Disneyland" (ABC)
Best Situation Comedy Series: "Make Room for Daddy" (ABC)

1955
Best Dramatic Series: "Producers' Showcase" (NBC)

Best Variety Series: "The Ed Sullivan Show" (CBS)

Best Comedy Series: "The Phil Silvers Show" (CBS)

1956

Best Series (half hour or less): "The Phil Silvers Show" (CBS)

Best Series (one hour or more): "Caesar's Hour" (NBC)

1957

Best Dramatic Series with Continuing Characters: "Gunsmoke" (CBS)

Best Dramatic Anthology Series: "Playhouse 90" (CBS)

Best Musical, Variety, Audience Participation, or Quiz Series: "The Dinah Shore Chevy Show" (NBC)

Best Comedy Series: "The Phil Silvers Show" (CBS)

1958–1959

Best Dramatic Series (one hour or longer): "Playhouse 90" (CBS)

Best Dramatic Series (less than one hour): "Alcoa-Goodyear Theatre" (NBC)

Best Musical or Variety Series: "The Dinah Shore Chevy Show" (NBC)

Best Comedy Series: "The Jack Benny Show" (CBS)

Best Western Series: "Maverick" (ABC)

Best Panel, Quiz, or Audience Participation Series: "What's My Line?" (CBS)

1959–1960

Outstanding Program Achievement in the Field of Humor: "The Art Carney Special" (NBC)

Outstanding Program Achievement in the Field of Drama: "Playhouse 90" (CBS)

Outstanding Program Achievement in the Field of Variety: "The Fabulous Fifties" (CBS)

1960–1961

Outstanding Program Achievement in the Field of Humor: "The Jack Benny Show" (CBS)

Outstanding Program Achievement in the Field of Drama: *Macbeth* ("Hallmark Hall of Fame") (NBC)

Outstanding Program Achievement in the Field of Variety: "Astaire Time" (NBC)

1961–1962

Outstanding Program Achievement in the Field of Humor: "The Bob Newhart Show" (NBC)

Outstanding Program Achievement in the Field of Drama: "The Defenders" (CBS)

Outstanding Program Achievement in the Field of Variety: "The Garry Moore
Show" (CBS)

1962–1963

Outstanding Program Achievement in the Field of Humor: "The Dick Van
Dyke Show" (CBS)

Outstanding Program Achievement in the Field of Drama: "The Defenders"
(CBS)

Outstanding Program Achievement in the Field of Variety: "The Andy
Williams Show" (NBC)

1963–1964

Outstanding Program Achievement in the Field of Humor: "The Dick Van
Dyke Show" (CBS)

Outstanding Program Achievement in the Field of Drama: "The Defenders"
(CBS)

Outstanding Program Achievement in the Field of Variety: "The Danny Kaye
Show" (CBS)

1964–1965

Outstanding Program Achievements in Entertainment: "The Dick Van Dyke
Show" (CBS); "The Magnificent Yankee" ("Hallmark Hall of Fame")
(NBC); "My Name Is Barbra" (CBS)

1965–1966

Outstanding Dramatic Series: "The Fugitive" (ABC)

Outstanding Variety Series: "The Andy Williams Show" (NBC)

Outstanding Comedy Series: "The Dick Van Dyke Show" (CBS)

1966–1967

Outstanding Dramatic Series: "Mission: Impossible" (CBS)

Outstanding Variety Series: "The Andy Williams Show" (NBC)

Outstanding Comedy Series: "The Monkees" (NBC)

1967–1968

Outstanding Dramatic Series: "Mission: Impossible" (CBS)

Outstanding Musical or Variety Series: "Rowan & Martin's Laugh-In" (NBC)

Outstanding Comedy Series: "Get Smart" (NBC)

1968–1969

Outstanding Dramatic Series: "NET Playhouse" (NET)

Outstanding Musical or Variety Series: "Rowan & Martin's Laugh-In"
(NBC)

Outstanding Comedy Series: "Get Smart" (NBC)

1969–1970
Outstanding Dramatic Series: "Marcus Welby, M.D." (ABC)
Outstanding Variety or Musical Series: "The David Frost Show" (syndicated)
Outstanding Comedy Series: "My World and Welcome to It" (NBC)
1970–1971
Outstanding Series—Drama: "The Senator" ("The Bold Ones") (NBC)
Outstanding Variety Series—Musical: "The Flip Wilson Show" (NBC)
Outstanding Variety Series—Talk: "The David Frost Show" (syndicated)
Outstanding Series—Comedy: "All in the Family" (CBS)
1971–1972
Outstanding Series—Drama: "Elizabeth R" ("Masterpiece Theatre") (PBS)
Outstanding Variety Series—Musical: "The Carol Burnett Show" (CBS)
Outstanding Variety Series—Talk: "The Dick Cavett Show" (ABC)
Outstanding Series—Comedy: "All in the Family" (CBS)
1972–1973
Outstanding Drama Series—Continuing: "The Waltons" (CBS)
Outstanding Variety Musical Series: "The Julie Andrews Hour" (ABC)
Outstanding Comedy Series: "All in the Family" (CBS)
1973–1974
Outstanding Drama Series: "Upstairs, Downstairs" ("Masterpiece
    Theatre")(PBS)
Outstanding Musical Variety Series: "The Carol Burnett Show" (CBS)
Outstanding Comedy Series: "M*A*S*H" (CBS)
1974–1975
Outstanding Drama Series: "Upstairs, Downstairs" ("Masterpiece Theatre")
    (PBS)
Outstanding Comedy, Variety or Music Series: "The Carol Burnett Show"
    (CBS)
Outstanding Comedy Series: "The Mary Tyler Moore Show" (CBS)
1975–1976
Outstanding Drama Series: "Police Story" (NBC)
Outstanding Comedy, Variety or Music Series: "Saturday Night Live" (NBC)
Outstanding Comedy Series: "The Mary Tyler Moore Show" (CBS)
1976–1977
Outstanding Drama Series: "Upstairs, Downstairs" ("Masterpiece
    Theatre")(PBS)

Outstanding Comedy, Variety or Music Series: "Van Dyke and Company" (NBC)

Outstanding Comedy Series: "The Mary Tyler Moore Show" (CBS)

1977–1978

Outstanding Drama Series: "The Rockford Files" (CBS)

Outstanding Comedy, Variety or Music Series: "The Muppet Show" (syndicated)

Outstanding Comedy Series: "All in the Family" (CBS)

1978–1979

Outstanding Drama Series: "Lou Grant" (CBS)

Outstanding Comedy Series: "Taxi" (ABC)

1979–1980

Outstanding Drama Series: "Lou Grant" (CBS)

Outstanding Comedy Series: "Taxi" (ABC)

1980–1981

Outstanding Drama Series: "Hill Street Blues" (NBC)

Outstanding Comedy Series: "Taxi" (ABC)

1981–1982

Outstanding Drama Series: "Hill Street Blues" (NBC)

Outstanding Comedy Series: "Barney Miller" (ABC)

1982–1983

Outstanding Drama Series: "Hill Street Blues" (NBC)

Outstanding Comedy Series: "Cheers" (NBC)

1983–1984

Outstanding Drama Series: "Hill Street Blues" (NBC)

Outstanding Comedy Series: "Cheers" (NBC)

1984–1985

Outstanding Drama Series: "Cagney & Lacey" (CBS)

Outstanding Comedy Series: "The Cosby Show" (NBC)

1985–1986

Outstanding Drama Series: "Cagney & Lacey" (CBS)

Outstanding Comedy Series: "The Golden Girls" (NBC)

1986–1987

Outstanding Drama Series: "L.A. Law" (NBC)

Outstanding Comedy Series: "The Golden Girls" (NBC)

1987–1988
Outstanding Drama Series: "thirtysomething" (ABC)
Outstanding Comedy Series: "The Wonder Years" (ABC)
1988–1989
Outstanding Drama Series: "L.A. Law" (NBC)
Outstanding Comedy Series: "Cheers" (NBC)
1989–1990
Outstanding Drama Series: "L.A. Law" (NBC)
Outstanding Comedy Series: "Murphy Brown" (CBS)
1990–1991
Outstanding Drama Series: "L.A. Law" (NBC)
Outstanding Comedy Series: "Cheers" (NBC)

Viewers can have more say about what they see on television. To voice your likes and dislikes or to suggest improvements, write to the networks listed here. Send your comments to the attention of the Audience Services Department.

To find the names and addresses of local stations (or of networks not named below), consult *Broadcasting Yearbook*, which is available in most public libraries.

OVER-THE-AIR NETWORKS

ABC, 77 West 66th Street, New York, NY 10023

CBS, 51 West 52nd Street, New York, NY 10019

Fox, Box 900, Beverly Hills, CA 90213

NBC, 30 Rockefeller Plaza, New York, NY 10112

PBS, 1320 Braddock Place, Alexandria, VA 22314

Telemundo, 1740 Broadway, New York, NY 10019

Univision, 9405 NW 41st Street, Miami, FL 33178

CABLE NETWORKS

Arts & Entertainment Network, 235 East 45th Street, New York, NY 10017

American Movie Classics, 150 Crossways Park West, Woodbury, NY 11797

Black Entertainment Television, 1232 31st Street NW, Washington, DC 20007

Bravo, 150 Crossways Park West, Woodbury, NY 11797

Cable News Network, One CNN Center, Box 105366, Atlanta, GA 30348

Cinemax, 1100 Avenue of the Americas, New York, NY 10036

Consumer News/Business Channel and Financial News Network, 2200 Fletcher Avenue, Fort Lee, NJ 07024

C-SPAN, 400 North Capitol Street NW, Washington, DC 20001

The Discovery Channel, 7700 Wisconsin Avenue, Bethesda, MD 20814

The Disney Channel, 3800 West Alameda Avenue, Burbank, CA 91505

ESPN, ESPN Plaza, Bristol, CT 06010

The Family Channel, 1000 Centerville Turnpike, Virginia Beach, VA 23463

Home Box Office, 1100 Avenue of the Americas, New York, NY 10036

Lifetime Television, 36-12 35th Avenue, Astoria, NY 11106

Madison Square Garden Network, 2 Penn Plaza, New York, NY 10121

The Movie Channel, 1633 Broadway, New York, NY 10019

Music Television, 1515 Broadway, New York, NY 10036

Nickelodeon, 1515 Broadway, New York, NY 10036

SportsChannel, 150 Crossways Park West, Woodbury, NY 11797

Showtime, 1633 Broadway, New York, NY 10019

Turner Broadcasting System, One CNN Center, Box 105366, Atlanta, GA 30348

Turner Network Television, One CNN Center, Box 105366, Atlanta, GA 30348

USA Network, 1230 Avenue of the Americas, New York, NY 10020

SELECT BIBLIOGRAPHY

^^

Television is the subject of an amazing amount of news and commentary in books, magazines, and newspapers. Below are a few selected sources from my research. *TV Guide, Variety,* the *New York Times,* and the trade magazine *Channels* alerted me to the latest news on the medium.

Several histories of television were invaluable. Erik Barnouw's *Tube of Plenty* (New York: Oxford University Press, 1975, 1982, 1990) is scholarly and pungent. J. Fred MacDonald's *One Nation Under Television: The Rise and Decline of Network TV* (New York: Pantheon, 1990) offered sharp insights. Also useful were *Television: The First Fifty Years,* by Jeff Greenfield (New York: Harry N. Abrams, 1977); *A Pictorial History of Television,* by Irving Settel (New York: Frederick Ungar, 1983); and *Watching TV: Four Decades of Television,* by Harry Castleman and Walter J. Podrazik (New York: McGraw-Hill Book Company, 1982). Michael Winship's *Television* (New York: Random House, 1988), a companion volume to the PBS series of the same name, deserves special mention for the quality of its interviews with television actors, producers, and other professionals.

The following are wonderful fact books about television: *The Complete Directory to Prime Time Network TV Shows, 1946–Present,* 4th edition, by Tim Brooks and Earle Marsh (New York: Ballantine Books, 1979, 1981, 1985, 1988); Cobbett Steinberg's *TV Facts* (New York: Facts on File, 1985); Stuart Fischer's *Kids' TV* (New York: Facts on File, 1982); and Vince Waldron's *Classic Sitcoms* (New York: Macmillan, 1987).

For insights into the business of television, I recommend *Inside Prime Time,* by Todd Gitlin (New York: Pantheon Books, 1983, 1985); *The Cool Fire,* by Bob Shanks (New York: W. W. Norton, 1976); and *Children's Television,* by Cy Schneider (Lincolnwood, IL: NTC Business Books, 1987).

Among the many works of social criticism about television, I found these constructive: *Changing Channels: Living (Sensibly) with TV,* by Peggy Charren and Martin W. Sandler (Reading, MA: Addison-Wesley, 1983); *The Plug-In Drug,* 2nd edition, by Marie Winn (New York: Viking Press, 1985); and *Media Speak,* by Donna Woolfolk Cross (New York: Coward-McCann, Inc., 1983).

Picture albums, "fan" books, and exposés have a solid place in television literature. I most enjoyed *Great Moments of Television,* by Thomas G. Aylesworth (New York: Exeter Books, 1987); *TV Book,* edited by Judy Fireman (New York: Workman Publishing, 1977); *Saturday Night: A Backstage History of "Saturday*

Night Live," by Doug Hill and Jeff Weingrad (New York: Beech Tree Books/
William Morrow, 1986); and John Javna's "Best of" series, which appears in my
Suggestions for Young Readers.

Of course, I also researched television by watching it—from "Nick at Nite"
reruns to the fine eight-part PBS series "Television." Finally, the Museum of
Television and Radio, located in New York, was a matchless source for programs
(such as "The Goldbergs") that exist only on archival tapes.

SUGGESTIONS FOR YOUNG READERS

Charren, Peggy, and Martin W. Sandler. *Changing Channels: Living (Sensibly) with TV*. Reading, MA: Addison-Wesley, 1983.

Collins, Max Allan, and John Javna. *The Best of Crime and Detective TV*. New York: Harmony Books, 1988.

Drucker, Malka, and Elizabeth James. *Series TV*. New York: Clarion/Ticknor & Fields, 1983.

Emmens, Carol A. *An Album of Television*. New York: Franklin Watts, 1980.

Jaspersohn, William. *A Day in the Life of a Television News Reporter*. Boston: Little, Brown, 1981.

Javna, John. *The Best of Science Fiction TV*. New York: Harmony Books, 1987.

————. *The Best of TV Sitcoms*. New York: Harmony Books, 1988.

Polk, Lee, and Eda LeShan. *The Incredible TV Machine*. New York: Macmillan, 1977.

Reed, Maxine K., and Robert M. Reed. *Career Opportunities in Television, Cable and Video*, 2nd ed. New York: Facts on File, 1986.

Seuling, Barbara. *You Can't Show Kids in Underwear and Other Little-Known Facts about TV*. Garden City, NY: Doubleday, 1982.

Winn, Marie. *Unplugging the Plug-In Drug*. New York: Viking Press, 1985.

INDEX

Page numbers of illustrations are in italics.

ABC (American Broadcasting Corporation). *See* Networks
Action for Children's Television (ACT), 107–108, 172
Advertising, 6, 7, 55, 97, 117–119, 128, 151
  on cable, 112, 135–137, 139, 141, 170–171
  and children, 99, 104, 107, 108, 168–170
  costs of, 95, 123–124, 125–127
  in other countries, 7, 149, 151
  regulation of, 107, 115–117
Affiliates, network, 6, 10, 12–13
African television, 148, 157
Agnew, Spiro T., 74
"All in the Family," 29, *30*, 127–128
"All My Children," *56*, 59
Allen, Steve, 64
Allison, Fran, 101–102, 108
American Academy of Pediatrics, 165, 166–167, 172
"America's Most Wanted," 83, *84*
"Amerika," 48, *163*
Animal programs, 102, *132*, 142
Arts & Entertainment Network (A&E), 35, 137, 140
Asian television, 148, 156–157
Audience. *See* Viewers

Ball, Lucille, 24–25, *26*
Barber, Walter Lanier "Red," 86–87, *88.*
Barnouw, Erik, xvi, 134
Baseball, 86–87, *88*, 94, 97, 98, *116*, 139
Basketball, 94–95
Beatles, the, 17, *19*
"Beauty and the Beast," 47, 127, 143
Berle, Milton, 13, 16–17, *18*

Blacklisting, 17, 43, *67–68*
Blanc, Mel, 106
Blank, Ben, 70
Blaya, Joaquin, 153
Blue-collar programs, 29, 31–33
Bochco, Steven, 41, 42
"Bonanza," 38, *40*, 148
Books, about television, *15*, 197–199
Boxing, 87, 97
Boycotts, to pressure sponsors, 118–119
Brain, changes in the, 162–164
Bravo, 137, 140
British television, 7, 149–150, 179
Buch, Frances, 12
Bush, President George, 79
Business, television as, 10, 75–77, 93–94, 104, 115–129
Butler, Owen B., 118–119

C-Span, 140, 180
Cable News Network (CNN), xiii, 11, 80–82, *81*, 148
Cable television, 11, 13, 121, 131, 135–139, 177–179
  addresses for networks, 195–196
  costs of, 117, 141, 144
  and kids' shows, 57–58, 109, 110–114
  and sports, 93, 97
Canadian television, 147, 148, 154
Caron, Glenn Gordon, 42
Carson, Johnny, 65
Carter, President Jimmy, 78, 93
Cartoons, 33, 104–110, 166
CBS (Columbia Broadcasting System). *See* Networks
Caeser, Sid, 17–20
Censorship, 17, 21–22, 82, 119, 165–166

Censorship (*cont.*)
  in other countries, 149
Characters, reality of, 38, 43, 59
Charren, Peggy, 107, 172
"Cheers," xv, 29, 120, 121–123, 127–
  128, 174
Chernin, Peter, 121
Children and young people, 57–58, 99–
  114, *100, 105, 111, 113,* 143, 150,
  162–166, 171–172
  and cable, 135–137, 141–142, 170–
  171
Children's Television Workshop, 103,
  104
Christian Broadcasting Network, 142,
  143
Civil rights, and television news, 71–73
"Civil War, The," 135, *136*
"Clarissa Explains It All," 110, *111*
CNBC/FNN, 137, 140
CNN. *See* Cable News Network
Coca, Imogene, 17–20
Color television, 9, 11, 73, 174
Comedy Central, 121, 141
Comedy programs, 17–33, 121–123
Commercials. *See* Advertising
Communists. *See* Blacklisting
Community access television (CATV).
  See Cable television
Computers, 176–177
Congress. *See also* FCC
  broadcast of proceedings, 12, 77–78
Consumers, 28, 125, 140, 166
  children as, 101, 168–170
Consumers Union, 168, 170
Cooney, Joan Ganz, 103
Corporations, 82–83, 137
  as sponsors, 97, 117–119, 134–135
"Cosby Show, The," xvi, *30,* 31, 121–
  123, 128
Costs, 144
  of advertising, 95–97, 117, 123–124,
  125
  of producing programs, 91–93, 98,
  128–129, 181

Coyle, Harry, 90
Crime shows, 83
Criticisms, of television, xiv, 99, 102,
  161– 172. *See also* Quality and lack
  of
Cronkite, Walter, xv, 71, 73

"Dallas," 61, 150
Damena, Kassaye, 148
Daytime television, 51–64
Delors, Jacques, 148
Demographics. *See* Viewers
Discovery Channel, the (TDC), 11, 112–
  114, 142
Disney Channel, the, 101, 112, 141–142
Docudramas, 48–50
Documentaries, 67–68, 75, 135
Donahue, Phil, 62
"Donna Reed Show, The," 25, 112, *122*
Dramas, 35–38, *49,* 61, 102, 110, *111,*
  181
Dramatizations, and television "news,"
  83, *84*
Du Mont network, 10, 87

EDTV (extended-definition television),
  176
Educational programs, 102–104, *105,*
  107, 133, 157, 170–171
Edwards, Douglas, 66–67
Edwards, Harry, 90
Eisenhower, President Dwight D., 68–
  70
Electricity, and invention of television, 4
Emmy award–winners, 43, 106, *126,*
  132, 189–194
Emotional impact of television, xiv, 36,
  48–50, 162
Equipment. *See* Technology
ESPN, 93, 137, 141, 148
European television, 7, 61, 147, 148,
  150–151, 174, 179
Exports, of American programs, 61, 148,
  150, 154, 158
Exposés, 67–68

Families, 172
  shows about, xiii, 24–28, 31–33, 47–48, 150
  shows for, 106, 112–114, 118–119
Family Chanel, the, 47, 112–114, 143
FCC (Federal Communications Commission), 6–7, 11, 57, 82, 165–166
  and cable, 97, 139, 141, 144
  educational programs, 107, 115–117, 133, 134
  and new stations, 10, 12–13, 180
Film studios, and television, 38, 106, 121
Foley, Archbishop John, 143
Football, 87, 89–90, 94, 95, 96
Ford Foundation, 133
Foreign language, imports to U.S., 158–159
Fox Network, xvi, 10, 11, 125
Franks, Martin D., 166
Freedman, Albert, 57
Frost, Mark, 42

Game shows, xii, 53–58, 54
Garroway, Dave, 51, 52
Gleason, Jackie, 24
Global village, xii–xiii
Gold, Herbert, 23
Golden Age of television, the, 35, 37
Government. See Congress; FCC
  control of television in other countries, 82, 148–149
"Green Acres," 27, 112, 120
Greenfield, Jeff, 38
Griffin, Merv, 57

Hadden, Jeffrey, 143
Hall, Arsenio, 65
HBO (Home Box Office), 11, 35, 109, 112, 137–139
HDTV (high-definition television), 174–176
Hennock, Frieda, 133
Henson, Jim, 101–102, 103, 104, 112
Herbert, Don, 102, 112
Herzog, Doug, 58

Hewitt, Don, 71, 75, 79, 180, 181–182
"Hill Street Blues," 41–42, 120
Hockey, 87, 94
"Honeymooners, The," 24, 173
"Howdy Doody," 12, 101, 108

"I Love Lucy," xiv, 24–25, 26
Ideas for programs, sources of, xvi, 57, 109, 119–120, 121
Imports, of foreign programs to U.S., 158–159
Independent stations. See Stations
Indian television, 156–157
Influence of television, xi, xvii, 162–164, 172
  social effects, xiii, 99, 164–168, 171–172
  on sports, 87, 90, 93–95, 141
Interactive television, 108, 177–179, 178
International television, 147–159
Invention of television, 3–4, 7
Iranian hostage crisis, 78, 93

Japanese television, 146, 154–156, 155, 174
Johnson, President Lyndon B., 71, 73

Kennedy, President John F., 70–71, 72
Kennedy, Senator Robert F., 73–74
Koppel, Ted, 78, 80
Kovacs, Ernie, 20, 64
Kraemer, Chuck, xiv
"Kukla, Fran and Ollie," 12, 101–102, 106, 108

"L.A. Law," xv, 40, 43, 147
Language, foreign, 147–148, 156–157, 158–159
Latin American television, 149, 151–153, 152, 160
Lawson, Jennifer, 131
Lawyer programs, 43
Lemmon, Jack, 36
Leno, Jay, 65
Letterman, David, 65

Licenses, broadcast, 13, 107, 115
Lippman, Andy, 174
Live television, 8, 20, 36, *37*, 38, 99–
    101
Local stations. *See* Stations
"Lou Grant," 28, 45
Low-power stations, 180
Lynch, David, 42

McCarthy, Senator Joseph, 17, 43,
    67–68
McLuhan, Marshall, xi–xii
"MacNeil/Lehrer NewsHour, The," 80,
    131
Marthesheimer, Peter, 50
"M*A*S*H," 29–31, 127–128
"Masterpiece Theatre," 131, 135
Medical programs, 43–45
"Meet the Press," 12, 67, 123
"Miami Vice," 42, 120, 150
Middle Eastern television, 156
Miniseries, 48–50, 125, 135
"Mister Rogers' Neighborhood," 103,
    134, 164–165
MIT Media Lab, 174, 176
Mohr, John, 97
Moon landing, 75, *76*
Moore, Mary Tyler, 28
Morning programs, 51–53
Morris, Bill, 90
Morris, Howard, 17–20
Movies, 36, 38, *49*, 137
    as source of program ideas, 31, 106,
    121
MTV (Music Television), 58, 80, 140–
    141, 148
Murrow, Edward R., xvii, 67–68, *69*
Music channels, 140–141
Myerson, Bess, *37*

Nader, Ralph, 180
Narrowcasting, 139–140
National Coalition on TV Violence, 166
NBC (National Broadcasting System).
    See Networks

Networks, 74–75, 79–82, 127, 129,
    179–180
    addresses for, 195
    and cable, 137, 139, 143–144
    competition among, xvi, 10, 28, 79–
    80, 123, 139, 181
    early years of, 4, 6, 8–9, 10
    self-policing of, 57, 119, 165–166
    and sports coverage, 87, 89, 91–93
News programs, xiv, 75–83, *85*, 125,
    180–181. *See also* Cable News Net-
    work
    children and young adult, *113*, 170–
    171
    dramatizations, 83, *84*
    early, 66–67, 70
Nickelodeon, 11, 110–112, *113*, 139,
    142
Nielsen ratings. *See* Ratings
Nixon, President Richard M., 21, 70–71,
    74, 77–78, 134
Nonprofit television, 7. *See also* PBS

O'Connor, John J., 31
OINKS, 31
Olympic Games, 91–93, *92*, 137
Operation Desert Storm, 80–82, *81*

Paar, Jack, 64–65
Paley, William S., 6
Pauley, Jane, xiii, 53, 129
PBS (Public Broadcasting Service), 35,
    80, 130–135, *132*, *136*, 159
    and kids' shows, 107, 109, 170–171
Persian Gulf war, 80–82, *81*
Pilot episodes, 120
Plays, 35–38, 135
Plug-In Drug, The, 162–165, 171
Police programs, 39–43
Politics, xv, 93
    campaigns, 68–71, 78–79, 142
    conventions, 67, 74
    and foreign television, 149, 150,
    153
Polskin, Harold, 31

Production
  of programs, 36, 119–120, 128, 159,
    181
Propaganda, in other countries, 149, 157
Protests, antiwar, 73, 74, 134
Public access channels, 135–137
Public-affairs programs, 67–68

Quality, picture, 174, 176
Quality in programming, and lack of, 36,
    104, 107, 115, 127
  and cable, 135–137, 141–142
Quiz shows. See Game shows

Race and prejudice, 17, 21, 31, 131,
    153, 156, *167*
Radio, 4–7, 16, 65, 156–157, 169
  influence on early television shows,
    20–21, 23–24, 38, 39, 58, 66–67
Rather, Dan, 74, 79, 129
Ratings, 93, 94, 108, 121, 123–128,
    135–137
  listing of top-rated programs, 185–
    187
"Ray Bradbury Theater," 137, *138*
RCA (Radio Corporation of America), 6,
    8, 9
Reagan, President Ronald, 78–79
Reality
  and television, xiii, xiv, 47–50, 59, 61,
    162
  blurring of, xv, 22, 28–31, 83, 181
Redford, Robert, 36
Reiner, Carl, 17–20
Relaxation, television as, xiv, 162
Religious programs, 142–143
Remote control, xii, 176
Reruns, 23, 112, 121, 128, 174, 181
Rivera, Geraldo, 62
Rivers, Joan, 65
Rogers, Fred, 103
"Roseanne," xiv, 31–33, 123, 147, 150
"Rowan & Martin's Laugh-In," 20,
    21–22
Royalties, for programs, 128–129

Safer, Morley, 75
Salaries
  and television, 90, 129
Sarnoff, David, 6, 8
Satellites, xvi, 139, 174, 179
  and news, 70, 82
"Saturday Night Live," 22–23, 121
Scandals, 55–57, *56*, 117–118, 142–
    143
Scheduling, 51, 67, 106–107, 109–110,
    117, 121–123
  early, 8, 11–12, 13
Science fiction programs, 46–47, *138*,
    145
Screens, television, 4, 173–174, *175*
Selection, of programs, 119–121, 127–
    128, 177, 181
Selling America's Kids, 168–169, 170
Serling, Rod, 46
"Sesame Street," 103–104, 130–131,
    134
Sex, on television, 118–119, 166–167
"Shining Time Station," *100*
Shopping channels, 140
Showtime, 11, 112–114
Silverman, Fred, 65, 120, 121, 179,
    181
"Simpsons, The," xvi, *33*, 34, 123
Sitcoms (situation comedies), 23–33
"60 Minutes," 75, 127–128
Soap operas, xiv, 12, 56, 58–61, 125,
    151–153
Social effects of television. See Influence
  of television
Sound bite, 78–79
South African television, 149, 156, 157
South American television, 61, 148
Soviet television, 148, 149, 158
Space program, 75, *76*, 80
Spielberg, Steven, 46–47, 109–110
Sports programs, 86–98, *88*, *92*, *96*,
    116
  and cable television, 137–139, 141
SportsChannel America, 93, 137, 141
"Square One Television," 104, *105*

Stations
  independent, 10–11, 12–13, 77, 82,
    126
  local, 6, 8, 10–11, 38, 82, 125,
    134
  low-power, 180
Stereotypes, xiii–xiv, 23, 29, 107
Stevenson, Adlai, 68
Subject matter, 29, 110, 135, 177
  controversial, xiv, 43, 48, 59, 118–
    119, 166–167
  relationships as, 38, 45
Sullivan, Ed, 17, *19*
Super Bowl, 94, 95–97, *96*, 123, 141
Superstations, 11
Swanson, Dorothy, 127
Swayze, John Cameron, 66–67
"Sweeps" months, 94, 125
Syndication, 128

Talk shows, 51–53, 62–65, *152*
Tartikoff, Brandon, 119–121
Technology, 89
  changes in, xv–xvi, 4, 9, 144, 173–
    177, *175*
  early production, 36, 38, 70
Telemundo, 10, 159
Telephone, and television, 3–4, 177
Televangelists, 142–143
Television sets, xii, 17
  costs of, 7, 9, *14*, 176
  production of, 8, 10, 11
Testing, on audiences, 120
"Texaco Star Theater," 17, 117
Third World television, 148, 151–153,
    156–157
"Tic Tac Dough," *54*, 55–57, *56*
Time, xii
  spent watching television, xii, 125,
    154
"Today," xiii, 51–53, *52*

Toys, and kids' television, 107, 108,
    168–170
Trudeau, Garry, 22–23
Turner, Ted, xiii, 80, 114
Turner Broadcasting System (TBS), 137,
    139
"Twin Peaks," 42–43, 120–121

Univision, 10, 159

Values, 117–118
  effect of television on, xiv, 17
Van Doren, Charles, 55, 57
Variety shows, 12, 16–21, 101, 153
Vaudeville, 16, 21
VCRs (videocassette recorders), xii, xvi,
    61, 127, 172, 176
Vietnam War, 21–22, 29, 31, 82, 134
  and television news, 73, 77
Viewers, 125
  demographics of, 28, 61
  habits of, xi–xii, xiv, 172
  influence of, 118–119, 166, 195–196
  number of, 95, 124–127, 171
Viewers for Quality Television, 127
Violence, 118–119, 150, 165–166, *167*
  amount of, 39, 107
  reducing, 73–75, 108, 133
VNRs (video news releases), 82–83

Watergate, broadcast of Senate hearings,
    77–78
Westerns, 38–39, *40*, 74–75
"Wheel of Fortune," *40*, 57
Winfrey, Oprah, 62–64, *63*
Winn, Marie, 162–165, 166, 171
Wire services, and news, 82
Wolper, David, 48, 91
"Wonder Years, The," 25–27, 118
Workplaces, sitcoms about, 28–29
World War II, effects of, 9–10, 11